Strategic Public Management

Best Practices from Government and Nonprofit Organizations

Strategic Public Management

Best Practices from Government and Nonprofit Organizations

Edited by
Howard R. Balanoff
Warren Master

ﬀﬀ
MANAGEMENTCONCEPTS

ｆｆｆ
MANAGEMENTCONCEPTS

8230 Leesburg Pike, Suite 800
Vienna, VA 22182
(703) 790-9595
Fax: (703) 790-1371
www.managementconcepts.com

Printed in the United States of America

Library of Congress Cataloging-in-Publication Data

Strategic public management : best practices from government and nonprofit organizations / edited by Howard Balanoff, Warren Master.

   p. cm.
     ISBN 978-1-56726-276-6
1. Local government. 2. Local government—United States. 3. Public administration. 4. Public administration—United States.   I. Balanoff, Howard R.   II. Master, Warren.
   JS78.S85 2010
   351—dc22

                        2009048306

10   9   8   7   6   5   4   3   2   1

About the Editors

Howard R. Balanoff is a professor of political science at Texas State University. He is also the chair of the university's William P. Hobby Center for Public Service and serves as the director of the Texas Certified Public Manager (CPM) program. He is the author of numerous articles on public administration and planning and is the editor of the textbook *Public Policy and Administration*. He is currently chair of the American Society for Public Administration's (ASPA) section for certified public management. Balanoff is a former member of ASPA's National Council and a former president of the National Certified Public Manager Consortium. He has also served as chair of ASPA's International Affairs Committee and chair of ASPA's section on professional and organizational development.

Balanoff's specialty areas are personnel administration, public policy, organizational theory and behavior, human resources administration, and professional development and education in the public sector. He holds the rank of Major USAF-Retired. Balanoff received a bachelor of arts in political science and history from Hunter College of the City University of New York. He received his master's degree and doctorate in urban and regional planning from Texas A&M University.

Warren Master is president and editor-in-chief of *The Public Manager* and has written and spoken regularly; planned conferences, forums, and related events; and conducted training workshops on strategic management and workplace innovation for the past 35 years.

Master's career in public service extends back to the mid-1960s when he and his wife served as Peace Corps volunteers in Turkey. Having served more than 29 years as a career manager in the federal government, 18 as a senior executive, he held a variety of high-level policy, program management, and administrative posts in diverse agency cultures. Including the Department of Health and Human Services (HHS), where he held positions of acting assistant secretary of Human Development Services (HDS), both acting commissioner and career deputy commissioner of the Administration for Children, Youth, and Families, director of HDS's Office of Policy Development, and chief of the Health Care Financing Administration's Bureau of Quality Control; the Office of Economic Opportunity; and the U.S. General Services Administration (GSA), where he led cross-servicing and workplace of the future programs. He also served collaterally as a senior consultant and leader of a variety of management improvement initiatives of the National Performance Review.

After leaving the government, Master formed his own consulting firm and led an interagency study group for the National Academy of Public Administration (NAPA) on linking administrative support with mission results to meet the requirements of the Government Performance and Results Act of 1993. He consulted with the U.S. Agency for International Development (USAID), including intensive on-site work in Nigeria and Bosnia and engagements with USAID's Africa and Management bureaus. He also consulted with the Department of Veterans Affairs, Federal Aviation Administration, and U.S. Customs Service. Later, he joined the public accounting and consulting firm of Clifton Gunderson, LLP, as director of Public Management Consulting. This new practice focused principally on client agency needs for improved accountability, productivity, and organization performance, including organizations at all levels of government, nonprofit entities, and developing nations and emerging democracies overseas.

About the Authors

Alan P. Balutis is director and distinguished fellow in Cisco Systems' Internet Business Solutions Group. He has spent more than 30 years in public service and industry leadership roles and is a founding member of the Federal CIO Council. He led its strategic planning and outreach committees, helped create the council's e-government committee, and served as its first chair. His 27 years in the federal sector were spent at the Department of Commerce, where he headed the management and budget office for over a decade and was its first CIO, and at the Department of Health, Education and Welfare (now the Department of Health and Human Services). He is also a fellow of the National Academy of Public Administration and is chairman of *The Public Manager* Board of Directors. He can be reached at abalutis@cisco.com.

Sheila Beckett is an intermittent international budget advisor and consultant. She previously served as a resident advisor for the budget and financial accountability program with the U.S. Department of Treasury's Office of Technical Assistance and was assigned to the Republic of Macedonia's Ministry of Finance for three years. Prior to that, she assisted the Ministries of Finance in both Serbia and Montenegro on budget matters. Beckett previously served as executive director of the Employees Retirement System of Texas (ERS), managing an investment portfolio with a market value of nearly $20 billion. She also served in a variety of budget positions spanning over 20 years in Texas state government, including budget director to both the governor and lieutenant governor.

Bart Bevers was appointed by Governor Rick Perry in 2007 as the Inspector General for the Texas Health & Human Services Commission—Office of Inspector General. He oversees activities involving fraud, abuse and waste in Texas' health and human services systems and supervises over 655 employees in 31 cities across the state. Bevers began his career in law enforcement in 1995 working for the Dallas County District Attorney's Office, where he was the Chief Prosecutor in five different criminal courts. He also serves on the Board of Regents for the Association of Certified Fraud Specialists (ACFS), the Board of Directors for the Association of Inspectors General (AIG), and is an instructor for the National White Collar Crime Center (NW3C). He is certified as a Certified Fraud Specialist by the Association of Certified Fraud Specialists, Certified Homeland Security, Level III (C.H.S-III) by the American Board of Certification in Homeland Security, Certified Inspector General by the Association of Inspectors General, and Certified Public Manager (CPM) by the American Academy of Certified Public Managers. Bevers is also licensed to practice law in Texas.

Anthony Bingham is president and CEO of the American Society for Training & Development (ASTD), the world's largest association dedicated to workplace learning and performance professionals. ASTD offers programs and services to help members improve individual and organizational performance through its 133 chapters in the United States and 30 international partner organizations that convene at local and regional levels throughout the world. Bingham also is the coauthor of *Presenting Learning,* released in April 2007. With broad-based business, financial, operational, and technical management expertise, Bingham joined ASTD in 2001 as the chief operating officer/chief information officer. He became president and CEO in February 2004. He can be reached at www.astd.org.

Aaron B. Corbett is an associate at McManis & Monsalve Associates and holds a master's degree in public administration from The George Washington University.

Dale R. Fleming directs strategic planning and operational support for San Diego County's Health & Human Services Agency. This division manages the agency's strategic planning, performance measurement, and operational evaluation efforts for all health and social services. In addition, she leads operational support services for healthcare access and self-sufficiency programs for the county. She is a 2009 recipient of the YWCA's Tribute to Women in Industry Award (TWIN), San Diego.

Toby Hammett Futrell has 32 years of experience in public administration, beginning as she rose through the ranks from an entry-level position with the City of Austin organization to become its top executive. As City Manager, she performed functions as diverse as human resources, parks, public health, finance, auditing, public works, utilities, and public safety. During this distinguished career, Futrell has worked on myriad major projects from economic development to environmental protection. She helped lead the initiatives that brought major employers to the City's Desired Development Zone and was instrumental in creating the thriving Second Street Retail District and Austin's Smart Growth initiative. Her cultural and recreational endeavors include winning the coveted national Gold Medal for Austin's parks system. Futrell earned an MBA from Southwest Texas State University. She taught political science at Texas A&M Corpus Christi University and is currently teaching through Texas State University's Certified Public Manager's Program.

Tracy Haugen is director of federal public services in human capital for Deloitte Consulting, LLP. She has worked in both the public and private sectors with domestic and international clients over the past nine years, implementing and adopting change for mission impact. Haugan has helped agencies cut through bureaucratic barriers using change techniques that connect people to deliver successful results. Recently, she hosted a half-day event, Best Practices for Making Government 2.0 Work Now with *Information Week*. She has also been interviewed by *Federal News Radio* on the topic of Gov 2.0. She can be reached at thaugen@deloitte.com or www.deloitte.com.

James Horton is currently a PhD candidate at the University of Texas at Arlington and has been employed in local government for the past 13 years. His research interests include local government management and performance improvement. He earned BS and MPA degrees from the University of North Texas and can be reached at james.horton@mavs.uta.edu.

Philip Kangas is a director within the Grant Thornton's Global Public Sector Organizational Improvement Team, working with federal clients to improve organizational performance through sourcing and acquisition management, business transformation, and human capital strategy consulting. He holds an MPA from the Syracuse University Maxwell School of Citizenship and Public Affairs and is certified by the Association of Government Accountability as a Certified Government Financial Manager (CGFM).

Peter McHugh is the CEO of Covalent Software Inc. He can be reached at peter.mchugh@covalentsoftware.com or www.covgov.com.

Nancy Fagenson Potok is the Deputy Under Secretary for Economic Affairs at the U.S. Department of Commerce. She was previously the chief operating officer of McManis & Monsalve Associates, a management consulting firm, and principal associate director and chief financial officer at the U.S. Census Bureau, among other senior executive positions in the public and private sector. Dr. Potok is a fellow of the National Academy of Public Administration and a recipient of the Arthur S. Flemming Award. She can be reached at npotok@doc.gov.

Alan R. Shark serves as the Public Technology Institute's executive director/CEO. He also serves as assistant professor at Rutgers University's School of Public Affairs and Administration. As an author, lecturer, and speaker on technology developments and applications for most of his distinguished career, Shark's experience both balances and embraces the business, government, education, and technology sectors. He has been elected as a Fellow of the National Academy of Public Administration (NAPA), as well as Fellow of the Radio Club of America (RCA) and Fellow of the American Society for Association Executives (ASAE). Shark holds a doctorate in public administration from the University of Southern California's Washington Public Policy Center and is the author of *Beyond e-Government & e-Democracy: A Global Perspective*. He can be reached at shark@pti.org.

Robert Shea is a director within the Grant Thornton Global Public Sector Cost and Performance Team and coordinates the firm's Recovery Act services. He has trained hundreds of federal employees on Recovery Act compliance. He was most recently at the U.S. Office of Management and Budget as associate director for Administration and Government Performance. Shea is a fellow and a member of the Board of Directors of the National Academy of Public Administration (NAPA).

Robert Shick is an assistant professor at the Rutgers-Newark School of Public Affairs and Administration, managing director of the National Center for Public Performance, and director of the Executive MPA Program. He has extensive experience in the public sector as a senior administrator in New York City government, working on contracting policy and implementation, and received his PhD in public administration from New York University. Shick's research interests include privatization and the contracting-out of government services, nonprofit management, and organizational development. He can be reached at rshick@andromeda. rutgers.edu.

James H. Thurmond is director of the MPA program and clinical professor at the University of Houston, where he teaches administrative theory, urban management, and comparative public policy. He retired from city government in 2003 after 30 years, including tours as director of community development with the City of Denison, Texas, and city manager of Cleveland, Uvalde, and Missouri City, Texas. He served two years in the U.S. Army, including 14 months in Vietnam, and has a PhD from the University of Houston and an MPA from the LBJ School of Public Affairs, University of Texas at Austin. He can be reached at jhthurmond@uh.edu.

William Trahant is a senior business consultant with extensive knowledge of strategic human capital planning issues, having consulted widely to cabinet-level federal government agencies and Fortune 500 corporations. The coauthor of several books, including *Business Climate Shifts: Profiles of Change Makers,* he most recently led the Government Consulting Services Practice of Watson Wyatt Worldwide. Trahant speaks frequently on human capital issues before public sector audiences and writes on human capital topics for publications such as *Government Executive, Federal Times,* and *The Public Manager.* He can be reached at Wtrahant@aol.com.

Jackie Werth is a project coordinator within the Office of Strategy Management, Health and Human Services Agency, San Diego County. She facilitates workshops, conducts analyses, and coordinates a wide range of projects to address performance challenges or advance strategic initiatives. Formerly, she served as senior evaluator for the U.S. General Accounting Office in Washington, D.C., where she received the Assistant Comptroller General's Award for excellence and community service. She can be reached at Jackie.Werth@sdcounty.ca.gov

Tim E. Winchell, Sr., is a retired federal human resources professional and president of Winchell Global Human Resources Consulting Services, LLC. He is currently working for a large consulting firm in the Washington, D.C., area and serves on the adjunct faculty of George Mason University and the Board of Editors of *The Public Manager.* He can be reached at TWinc33551@aol.com.

Contents

Editors' Preface

Over the past decade or so, government at all levels has begun requiring short- and long-term plans, including strategic goals, measurable objectives, a system for assessing outcomes, and periodic reporting on results. More recently, decisionmakers have attempted to tie budget and other resource decisions to agency performance.

Ironically, this shift to a more results-oriented management system has not had a noticeable effect on public-sector organizational culture. Such a transformation would surely have nudged organizations out of their bureaucratic silos and stovepipes, where behavioral changes would be apparent.

Numerous basic books and training materials that present the fundamentals of public management are available. A variety of books and journals address more abstract and theoretical issues, and a few periodicals are aimed at explicating and sharing best practices in response to some of the more vexing challenges confronting public-sector practitioners around the world today. Typically, these publications are written with an eye toward a particular community of practice (e.g., human resources, budget and finance, acquisition and procurement).

In recognition that the aim of public service is the highest level of performance possible, this book addresses the challenges and solutions that all aspects of an organization—indeed, the family of public-sector organizations—face. The 17 chapters of this strategically oriented public management book are intended to serve the needs of both mid- and senior-level practitioners as well as academics involved in applied research or who teach public administration at the undergraduate and graduate levels.

In a multisector workforce—one populated by career and non-career employees, political appointees, and contractor staff—we offer this book as a guide to navigating cross-boundary goals and challenges.

From their own particular perspectives, the authors of this book explore the extent to which key elements of public-sector entities—staff and line, headquarters, and field—have become sufficiently integrated with the larger organization's strategic planning and management system. They consider a wide spectrum of issues and challenges: How can the highly segmented silos of bureaucratic subcultures be transformed so that they regularly collaborate in meeting common challenges? How are technologists, acquisition officials, budget and financial managers, human capital leaders, program operations staff, and other policy development officials working together to achieve priority strategic goals? How are all government agency players held accountable for meeting outcome requirements at periodic performance reporting meetings? How do they all get a seat at the table? How can contractors (e.g., private-sector vendors, public nonprofits, nongovernmental organizations [NGOs]) also be held accountable for meeting outcome requirements? How can we ensure that all network participants serve as strategic members of the organization's team?

How This Book Is Organized

To frame this discussion, we have grouped the chapters of this book into five broad areas of responsibility found in virtually all public management settings:

- **Part 1: Strategic Program Operations:** Planning and managing core mission functions to maximum effect

- **Part 2: Strategic Budget and Financial Management:** Accountability

- **Part 3: Strategic Human Capital Management:** Recruiting, developing, and utilizing people effectively

- **Part 4: Strategic Knowledge and Technology Management:** Absorbing and benefiting from new technologies

- **Part 5: Strategic Acquisition Management:** Balancing and controlling sourcing.

In addition, the book addresses one overarching concern that should be part of any successful public management repertoire:

- **Part 6: Strategic Performance Management:** Pursuing measurable results.

Each chapter within these six parts offers perspectives from different levels of government and a variety of programmatic and occupational settings. The authors of each chapter share their unique experiences, offering insights and guidance that we believe public management practitioners will find directly relevant—and applicable—to their own environments and situations.

Part 1: Strategic Program Operations

With respect to planning and managing basic mission-linked line programs and related administrative support functions (e.g., facilities, purchasing, fleet), how can people working within previously entrenched bureaucratic cultures share responsibility for achieving results? What are different levels of government (and the nonprofit/NGO community) doing to prepare for and respond more collaboratively to catastrophic disasters? How are lessons learned and new techniques in one setting institutionally shared with others? How have government and public nonprofit organizations worked together successfully internationally and in other cross-cultural environments?

Chapter 1: Kicking off this discussion, **James H. Thurmond** shares his experiences and reflections on planning and managing core mission functions at the municipal level. Drawing from his more than 30 years of public service at the local level, including his work as director of community development and city manager in a number of towns in the Southwest, Thurmond explores how local government managers respond to major problems in an interdependent world. He probes whether they look outward beyond their organizations to identify and diagnose problems and to understand their contours, causes, and interrelated parts. He suggests that a best practice is to conceptualize the problem from a perspective that is both internally and externally focused.

Chapter 2: Next, **Jackie Werth** and **Dale R. Fleming** offer their perspective on planning and managing core mission functions in San Diego County, California, particularly in the context of several major initiatives of the county's Health & Human Services Agency (HHSA). Reflecting on their years of experience in strategic and operational planning and complex project coordination at the local level, as well as Werth's tour as senior evaluator for the U.S. General Accountability Office (GAO), the authors demonstrate how strategic alignment—variations of business process review (BPR)—have helped organizations improve performance and work effectively within increasingly constrained budgets.

Chapter 3: Rounding out this discussion of strategic program operations, **Tim E. Winchell, Sr.,** provides insight into planning and resource decision-making at the federal level. Given his experience in the federal government and years of research, classroom instruction, and consulting, he finds an increased emphasis on strategic planning, team-based problem-solving, and customer-focused program assessment. Nonetheless, classic command-and-control structures remain in place in many agencies. While internal agency cultures vary markedly, management planning and resource allocation processes are surprisingly consistent and have changed little over decades. Winchell identifies the structural and regulatory bases for these behaviors and offers recommendations for enhancing federal productivity.

Part 2: Strategic Budget and Financial Management

In the area of budget and finance, as agency responsibilities have grown in size and complexity, how have agency strategic emphases shifted to address priority oversight needs? Performance measurement aside, what pressing demands must be addressed in the area of financial ethics, particularly in terms of deeply entrenched assumptions and organizational behavior, and how are organizations responding? In recent years, government organizations have been required to address a wide range of administrative and programmatic risks in the management of their mission responsibilities. What new technologies, tools, and techniques are being used to assess and mitigate risks and ensure proper internal controls? Given the increased emphasis on performance measurement and the attempt to tie budget and other resource decisions to agency performance, how are organizations managing and sharing costs and employing more results-oriented budgeting techniques?

Chapter 4: Getting us started in this area, **Nancy Fagenson Potok** and **Aaron B. Corbett** lay out the landscape for managing risk in the highly interdependent federal fiscal environment. Based on Potok's senior-level fiscal experience in the federal government and both authors' research and consulting with public-sector organizations, they explore the processes of identifying, analyzing, measuring, and controlling risks within an agency's standards of acceptability. They focus on the three phases of risk management: identification, measurement, and management.

Chapter 5: Extending the topic of risk management and fast-forwarding to a priority concern early in the Obama administration, **Robert Shea** and **Philip Kangas** hone in on minimizing risk in the federal government's economic stimulus efforts by avoiding fraud, waste, and abuse in recovery project spending. With oversight responsibilities spread across the Recovery Accountability and Transparency Board, GAO, agency-level inspectors general, the White House, and ultimately citizens (through www.recovery.gov), external scrutiny will be intense. How should agencies, already stretched thin by copious audit, investigation, and reporting requirements, go about tackling these new and ambitious responsibilities?

Chapter 6: Sheila Beckett shares her recent fiduciary leadership experience in managing a very large, complex, and dynamic governmental health plan. The Group Benefits Program is one of the most successful programs in Texas state government. It is the health plan that others attempt to emulate and other groups of public-sector employees seek to join. Beckett presents several reasons the program has been able to sustain this reputation: its emphasis on the customer, balanced with fiscal responsibility; global coverage; frequent communication and collaboration with all financial partners and other key stakeholders; a good contracting process for retaining private-sector partners; transparency and regular disclosure to government and legislative leaders, employee and retiree groups, and the press; and a credible and effective formal appeals process for the denial of health benefits.

Part 3: Strategic Human Capital Management

The human capital challenge is framed by new demographics and the need to recruit, engage, and retain young professionals. Considering the anticipated departure of a high percentage of baby boomers over the next three to five years (including many from the senior ranks of government's career leadership) and the difficulty of attracting younger generations to public service, what are organizations doing to address this challenge in each occupational segment of the workforce? How are workplace learning efforts focusing on measuring performance and linking pay and performance? Given the complexity, wide variety, and pressing nature of the challenges facing today's government organizations, what are agencies doing to prepare their current and future leaders and managers to drive change over the next several decades? How do these strategies cut across entrenched organizational subcultures? And what needs to be done to avoid throwing out the baby with the bathwater—issues of ethics, accountability, and flexibility in the face of hard times?

Chapter 7: Based on years of observing trends through his research and consulting, **William Trahant** offers a road map for federal strategic human capital planning. He notes that increasingly, federal agencies are developing strategic human capital plans to help them meet changing mission requirements and ensure a purposeful, long-term approach. He describes the factors that are critical for a federal agency to implement strategic human capital planning effectively. Trahant presents a comprehensive, structured approach to assessing an organization's current and long-term human capital needs, with strategies and actions aimed at meeting those needs.

Chapter 8: Based on his years of experience in the area of public-sector practitioner training and education, **Howard R. Balanoff** provides an overview of the strategic role that Certified Public Management (CPM) programs play in integrating professional development efforts for public and nonprofit managers. Woven throughout this chapter are examples of how some states and local communities have creatively begun to use CPM coursework and certification to improve organizational performance as well as to retain young professionals by rewarding public-service career paths.

Chapter 9: Balancing the need for change with the traditional emphasis on ethics and accountability, **Bart Bevers** recounts avoidable misadventures in personal behavior that illustrate a common threat to public trust right within our own organization boundaries. He offers some practical takeaways on ethical values and principles and how they can be applied to an enduring, normative system of decision-making.

Chapter 10: In her chapter on creating a healthy workplace culture while managing deficits and downturns in Austin, Texas, **Toby Hammett Futrell** underscores the importance of the public manager's influence on corporate culture during the turmoil of downsizing. Her prescription: the three Cs–communication, control, and change. She believes that "...for a public manager, the 'brass ring' is forging an effective partnership with employees," and she offers concrete examples of tools available to most of us that can serve as vehicles for succeeding on these fronts. These include town hall meetings, rumor control hotlines, employee workforce committees, focus groups and straw polls, celebrations, and other additions to the manager's customary repertoire.

Chapter 11: Given his pivotal role as head of this country's premier training and development professional society, **Anthony Bingham** offers his thinking and suggestions on why talent matters and what public-sector agencies can do to maximize their talent strategically and systemically. He notes that a recent study identified the best practices of effective talent management and the tactics most strongly associated with success as driving talent management from the top of the organization to ensure its support by senior management; ensuring that talent management efforts support key agency strategies; aligning all components of talent management to support optimal performance; managing talent management with a long-range perspective, but with the ability to respond to changes in capability requirements as needed; and using talent-management metrics.

Part 4: Strategic Knowledge and Technology Management

How do agency strategies ensure that organizations will keep pace with new technologies and the rising expectations of all relevant users—citizens, the business community, and a younger, more web-savvy workforce? How will government 2.0 potentially transform the public-sector landscape as it becomes a priority for the Obama administration? How are government agencies taking advantage of virtual office technologies while addressing cybersecurity issues and other emerging public-sector challenges? What are agencies doing to incorporate telework and other flexible workplace arrangements, and how can these efforts be integrated into a larger initiative to evolve the workplace of the future? How will agency initiatives help transcend the boundaries of federal, state, and local governments and foster collaboration among the public, private, and nonprofit sectors? And how are government agencies engaging citizens today, particularly in the context of new communication technologies?

Chapter 12: Alan P. Balutis uses his considerable senior-level experience as a former federal chief information officer (CIO) and more recent professional IT management roles in the private and nonprofit sectors to frame the technology challenges for 21st-century government. He points out that the current administration is building on and expanding e-government initiatives, increasing government's openness and transparency, making use of Web 2.0 collaborative tools, and exploring cloud computing and other mechanisms to reduce infrastructure investments. Moreover, technology is now seen as an enabler that helps organizations deal with major challenges in such policy arenas as health, transportation, energy, and the environment. Encouraging signs include federal agencies harnessing new technologies to publish online information about their operations and decisions in ways that are readily available to the public; providing better levels of transparency and openness and devising new tools to let citizens participate and have their voices heard; and supporting workers' expectations that the same productivity, multitasking, and mobility tools they grew up with at home will also be in their workplace.

Chapter 13: Next, as an observer of technology developments and applications for most of his distinguished career, **Alan R. Shark** reflects on webcentricity and highlights challenges for public management. He explores the enormous power, pitfalls, and possibilities of integrating webcentricity into government applications, noting the extensive planning, experimentation, exploration, and careful navigation that will be required. He cites five webcentric trends that public managers simply cannot ignore: the pocket computer/phone, transparency and citizen engagement, social networking phenomena, virtual and viral immediacy, and social and virtual presence.

Chapter 14: Complementing these perspectives on how technology presents both challenges and opportunities, **Tracy Haugen** makes the case for Web 2.0's knowledge-management potential in the public sector. She reminds us that many supporting players are involved in program execution—other agencies and jurisdictions (state, local, or foreign governments), the academic community, and nonprofits—and that these elements complicate the modern government work environment. The dynamic nature of the governmental workforce makes capturing the magnitude of the knowledge management challenge daunting. Knowledge managers must consider the different segments and sources of work products when designing a strategy that captures workers' tacit knowledge and encompasses the multisector workforce.

Part 5: Strategic Acquisition Management

Increasingly, government work requirements are sourced to private contractors. Given the need to measure and report on the performance of all parties, how are organizations communicating oversight and accountability roles and responsibilities in such a demanding, resource-stretched environment? How have government organizations successfully engaged the private sector, achieving high performance while remaining faithful to their missions and codes of ethics and protecting the proprietary needs of their business counterparts? Moreover, what is being planned to ensure performance measurement and distribute responsibility appropriately in a multisector workforce? What are agencies doing to achieve coherence in these blended workforce arrangements while complying with legislative, regulatory, and other stewardship requirements?

Chapter 15: Drawing on his extensive experience as a senior administrator focused on contracting policy and implementation in New York City government, **Robert Shick** examines contracting for services at the state and local levels. He addresses the state of contracting for services, focusing on the most important lessons learned over recent years. Shick believes that government contracting is a holistic process that encompasses interdependent elements, including the make-or-buy decision; the contract document; the solicitation and selection of contractors; contract administration; evaluation of contractor performance; and the use of contractor performance information to make future contracting decisions.

Part 6: Strategic Performance Management

The shift during the past decade or so to measuring outcomes and reporting on results has led to a more strategic focus on public-sector performance. To what extent have various government and public nonprofit organizations fostered a performance culture? How do they ensure that all contributors across the organization understand the link between the procurement process and vendor performance, as well as between setting budget priorities and justifying and reporting on measurable outcomes? Have organizations invested in training and development to compare their performance against common standards or to learn how other public-sector organizations use benchmarking and other methods to improve and evaluate performance? With respect to fostering an organization-wide performance culture, what efforts are being made to pass along lessons learned from other public-sector organizations?

Chapter 16: Given his experience at the local government level and research interest in performance management, **James Horton** contributes an in-depth look at Citistat, a cross-departmental program used to evaluate city management in Baltimore, Maryland. Citistat cities conduct frequent meetings using data to discuss past performance, future objectives, and performance strategies to accomplish those objectives. The major drivers of this strategic management method include the active engagement of the city's top executives; the timeliness and scope of the data; questioning, feedback, and follow-up; the consequences for good, poor, and improved performance; a focus on problem-solving, continuous experimentation, and learning; and the institutional memory of the city's top executives. Taken together as part of an integrated management system, these components provide a blueprint for city leaders.

Chapter 17: Based on first-hand experience in Europe and more recently in the southwestern part of the United States, **Peter McHugh** compares local-level performance management in the United Kingdom and United States. He notes that local United Kingdom governments have sharpened their performance management skills and in the process have developed a range of relevant tools and approaches that nurture a performance culture. McHugh focuses on six of these skill areas and contrasts the situation with that at the local level in the United States, namely creating a holistic performance management framework; aligning resources and activities with corporate goals; benchmarking against similar-profile organizations; performance reporting to citizens; tracking performance in partnerships; and using software to support the performance management process.

We expect that a significant number of readers will be practitioners currently enrolled in CPM programs around the country. The national CPM program is currently offered in 36 states throughout the United States (http://www.cpmconsortium.org). Also, through related networks and training and development programs that serve public-sector organizations worldwide, we anticipate that this book will be relevant to hundreds of thousands of other managers at all levels of government, the public nonprofit sector, and nongovernmental organizations.

Moreover, we are optimistic that a much larger community of practitioners, academics, students, and others in the consulting and training and development fields will find this book helpful. We believe it is particularly timely as everyone from government leaders to first responders seek to understand and solve management challenges in an increasingly interdependent and hopefully transparent environment.

Howard R. Balanoff
Warren Master
October 2009

Acknowledgments

The editors wish to thank all those who found the time in their busy schedules to contribute to this volume. We are indeed grateful for their thoughtful consideration of our request for a collaborative view of public management roles. Not only did these colleagues dig deep into their professional experiences to reflect on the techniques and wisdom that were worth passing along to others, but they indulged our iterative exchanges to tease out even more nuggets from their rich careers in public service, research, and teaching.

We also wish to thank Myra Strauss and Lena Johnson of Management Concepts—Myra for approaching us with the initial idea for the book and for her openness and flexibility, and Lena for further help with editing and accommodating the full range of devilish organizational details that come with the territory. Looking back on this enterprise, a pivotal moment was when the authors asked Myra's indulgence for allowing them to address the interrelatedness of contemporary public management challenges and solutions. And as Robert Frost once wrote, "That has made all the difference."

PART 1

Strategic Program Operations

CHAPTER 1 ————————————————

Planning and Managing Core Mission Functions at the Municipal Level

James H. Thurmond

How do local government managers respond when confronted with a major problem? Are they internally or externally focused? Is their response instinctively based upon their organization's functional and process-based work formats? For example, if street pothole repair sequentially requires a street repair policy, a budget line item, and a work order signed by a supervisor before the repair work occurs, do these formalities blind the public works team to seeing challenging problems that do not resemble its own functions and processes? Or does the team look outward, beyond the organization, to scan the landscape and the horizon? Does it identify and diagnose problems, striving to understand their contours, causes, and interrelated parts, and does it determine whether the problem is routine or challenging before deciding upon the proper response?[1]

The best practice for responding to a major problem—which may or may not represent a daunting challenge—is conceptualizing the problem before selecting a strategic response. Managers must conceptualize problems from a perspective that is both internally and externally focused.

What Is Conceptualization?

Conceptualization of a problem requires the ability to consider a problem from both internal and external perspectives. Internal conceptualization is not difficult because managers instinctively react to external events by focusing internally to protect their organizations and because most managers prefer their own organizations to provide public services directly. Consequently, managers more readily conceptualize problems internally.

Local government managers work in hierarchically structured public organizations shaped by typical characteristics of bureaucracy: vertical control, top-down communications, standardized procedures, and an internal focus on core functions such as public safety, utilities, streets, drainage, and public health. They strive to protect these core functions from external disturbances in the organizational environment, such as political turmoil, poor economic conditions, interference from other governmental organizations, and issues stemming from high uncertainty, by ensuring that the internal bureaucratic structures for providing the core public services, including standard operating procedures and routines, hierarchical authority, funding mechanisms, and easy access to organizational resources, remain intact.

Local government managers tend to prefer providing services that are internally produced by their own organizations, but this preference has been changing over the last three decades. Local governments have begun to rely more on externally produced services provided by private businesses, other governmental entities, and nonprofits. For example, very few city services were externally produced until the early 1980s; today, more than 40 percent of city services are provided externally.[2]

Internally produced services, however, remain managers' instinctive mode of delivery. That is, they consider the city organization as the producer of services first, before contemplating external mechanisms. This is not surprising because managers certainly have more control and power within their own organizations via hierarchical authority than they do outside their organizations. They also know that providing services directly is usually more efficient and less time consuming because the necessary processes, rules, authority, and resources—all of which facilitate managerial control—are already in place.

But by looking beyond the organization when problem-solving, managers avoid being locked into an internal focus that precludes the consideration of external solutions to a problem. Conceptualization enables managers to better understand whether their organizational capacities match up to the problem at hand and to determine whether there is a need for network partners outside their organizations that can help address the problem. Once the problem is identified either as one that can be handled internally or as a daunting challenge requiring external resources, the appropriate strategic managerial action can be readily chosen (see Figure 1-1).

Figure 1-1: Steps in Addressing a Problem

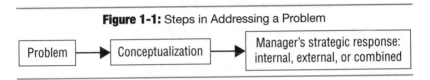

Solving Wicked Problems

Managers are confronted daily by challenges to their core services. Some challenges are relatively routine but still of sufficient magnitude to test the city's capacity. A three-alarm fire, a major water line break affecting a large section of the city, or a crime wave in the business sector are all problems that could strain a city's ability to respond. Usually, routine managerial practices and internal standard operating procedures, policies, guidelines, and existing resources are sufficient to manage even major problems. In other words, the single public organization can handle the challenge without outside assistance. Beyond these routine challenges, however, are the daunting challenges that are frequently described as "wicked"[3] because they have no apparent solution, they are multi-jurisdictional, and they seem to reoccur over time.

Handling wicked challenges is beyond the capacity of the single public organization and often transcends the legal territorial boundaries of the single organization. Wicked challenges are best addressed through a networked, multiorganizational approach external to the single organization. A *network* is an active, organized collaboration of organizations that accomplishes some agreed-upon purpose, and its key characteristic is interdependence between the participating organizations to perform a task.

It is essential for the manager to determine if the organization is truly experiencing a wicked problem before he or she can adequately address it. The manager must be able to conceptualize the problem both internally and externally, to switch between internal and external contexts, and to practice collaborative management.

Distinguishing Among Wicked Problems

Wicked problems are usually easily identified. They are multi-jurisdictional; for example, a natural disaster or metropolitan-wide traffic congestion are both wicked problems. Alternatively, higher levels of government or the courts may declare that a wicked problem exists and demand an external strategic response. This leaves local governments with little freedom to determine whether the problem is wicked or not.

Frequently, ambiguous wicked problems are the most problematic. They are less obvious at first glance because they appear to be routine and simple. Accordingly, managers' perspective on such problems is limited and project-oriented, and they do not recognize that the issues at hand are interrelated and intergovernmental, especially in a metropolitan area.[4]

Obvious Wicked Problem

Most public managers understand that a hurricane is a wicked problem and that they must look both internally and externally for responses to potential hurricane damage. Most realize that they should be prepared to handle most problems internally for the first 72 hours after the storm, then look externally, either for relief or to provide relief to others.

Those who take only an internal focus might be prepared for the first few hours of a hurricane and its immediate aftermath, but recovery would be hampered by the lack of external collaborative networks involving such entities as the county, private utility companies, the Federal Emergency Management Agency (FEMA), the state, nonprofits, for-profits, and neighboring cities. On the other hand, those whose focus is exclusively external might expect the state or federal government to provide relief right away, just as New Orleans managers did after Hurricane Katrina.

For an obvious wicked problem like a hurricane, managers can skip deciding whether a wicked problem exists. They should immediately begin conceptualizing the problem from a combined internal and external perspective, then decide on a strategic response.

Mandated Wicked Problem

The EPA required local governments to prepare and adopt a stormwater management program that included all stakeholders in the planning process, ensuring a broader organizational perspective for the plan. Under a mandate like this, managerial conceptualization and discretion are not needed to determine if a wicked problem exists or to choose an internal or external approach, because both the wicked problem and an external strategic response are mandated.

Ambiguous Wicked Problem

When the wicked problem is neither obvious nor mandated, external conceptualization is more important than ever because the manager must identify the parameters of the problem beyond his or her organization's boundaries. For example, the City of Southside Place in metropolitan Houston, Texas, planned a street reconstruction project that could have been considered just a simple project with limited ramifications. The city might have failed to conceptualize the external aspects of the problem, but fortunately, the city's consulting engineer also worked for the neighboring City of West University Place and had performed a drainage study for both cities. Based on the engineer's information about other jurisdictions, the city managers of both cities took a more holistic view and determined that the simple street project was more complex than it seemed. They realized that both cities could benefit if a larger drainage system planned by the Harris County Flood Control District were included in the Southside Place street project. There were also drainage advantages to be gained by both cities by replacing a bridge that belonged to the City of Houston.

As the project evolved, Houston recognized an opportunity to replace a major water transmission line along the Southside Place street. Ultimately, what began as a simple street project for only Southside Place became a partnership with West University Place, the City of Houston, and the Harris County Flood Control District—and a cost-effective solution that benefited all parties was implemented.

If Southside Place had undertaken the street work without collaborating with the other entities, the work would have amounted to nothing but a costly interim solution. The street would have been demolished and rebuilt twice more—once for the larger stormwater drainage line and once for Houston's water transmission line. What seemed like a simple project when all the facts were not known became a wicked problem requiring external strategic actions from the public managers of several governmental entities.[5]

As discussed previously, an external focus is not easy. Local government managers are implementers who naturally look to their single organizations to solve problems. This inherent internal focus can lead to failure to understand the problem, its external dimensions, and the limits of organizational capacity. Consequently, managers miss potential external solutions and increase their potential for failure.

Failure to Conceptualize Externally

An example of managerial failure to properly conceptualize a problem occurred in Missouri City, Texas, in the late 1990s. Over a 25-year period, the city had allowed the incorporation of 18 special districts, called *municipal utility districts* (MUDs), within the city limits. These MUDs provided water and wastewater services to more than 50,000 residents— with what the city considered to be an abundance of duplicative services and inefficiencies. When the city council considered consolidating the 18 MUDs, I recommended the *single city organization approach*—that is, an internal organizational focus based on the ideas that bigger is better (and "bigger" allowed economies of scale) and that the city could do it all.

This idea had disastrous consequences for the city council (three council members were defeated for reelection), and the mayor ultimately withdrew the policy proposal from the agenda because of its divisiveness in the community. Basically, the city pushed the policy proposal over the opposition of the MUD elected officials and some very vocal citizens and did not consider a collaborative solution to the problem.

If I had conceptualized the problem externally, I would have better understood the political realities at hand: the opinions of the almost 100 elected officials on the 18 MUD boards and numerous MUD consultants, as well as opposition from citizens, who considered the plan to be another example of "big government." I had conceptualized the solution strictly as an internal city operation that could be absorbed into the existing city organization as a separate department with improved economies of scale. While technically I may have been right regarding economies of scale and savings, my internal conceptualization and its single organizational approach was not feasible for such a politically complex situation. This was certainly a failure to properly conceptualize the problem.

Small Problems and Conceptualization

Conceptualizing also applies to small problems and can facilitate greater success. In Uvalde, Texas, a nonprofit agency, the Uvalde Recreational Council (URC), had long organized and managed a summer youth program in conjunction with the city. Initially, from an internally focused perspective, I thought that using the URC for such a limited, seasonal purpose was burdensome and time-consuming for the city of Uvalde. When I conceptualized the URC's role from an external, broader community perspective, I reached a different conclusion. Because the URC had credibility in the community, its involvement encouraged and facilitated community participation. It also was eligible for United Way funds, which could be combined with city funds.

While this was not a wicked problem in one sense—the city did not lack the resources to address the problem—my collaborative response helped address a deeper sustainability challenge. That is, I had no hierarchical control over the URC, interdependence existed between the city and the URC, and I used collaborative management skills. From a strictly internal organizational perspective, the city could have run the summer program alone, but at increased financial cost and with less community support. By conceptualizing the external environment, I found external benefits that outweighed the benefits of providing services internally.

Managers' Capacity to Implement Solutions

Conceptualization of the problem and the selection of the best strategic response, whether internal, external, or combined, are not sufficient unless managers possess two prerequisite capacities: the managerial agility and collaborative skills to implement the solution.

Once managers identify the context in which they are managing, they must adjust their roles and behaviors accordingly. They must work inside the organization and outside the organization. They cannot manage with only an internal management mindset or an external mindset. They must be able to transition between these internal and external contexts and to work in each specific context, sometimes simultaneously. Agile managers strategically match their responses with the organizational context[6] by integrating competing viewpoints, maintaining low levels of dogmatism, and being open-minded.[7]

It is no longer sufficient, if it ever was, for a manager to possess only internal organizational skills. Collaborative skills help the manager work external to his or her organization, where there is little hierarchical authority and the manager's internal organizational authority has limited impact. *Collaborative management* is basically the process of facilitating and operating in networked arrangements to solve problems that cannot be solved or easily solved by a single organization.

Collaborative management skills include bargaining, facilitating, mediating, arranging, empowering other participants, persuading others, and team building,[8] as well as managing conflict, power, leadership, building trust, negotiating, diplomacy, and inspiring others.[9] Specifically, when working externally, managers must be able to identify participants who will help achieve the network's goals; facilitate agreement on leadership and administrative roles in the network; establish an identity and culture for the network; induce commitment to the network; and engender productive interaction among network participants.[10]

Managers work in hierarchical organizations, and they instinctively focus internally on problems. This is not necessarily inappropriate for routine problems that can be addressed with organizational resources and procedures, but for wicked problems requiring external resources, it can result in poor public policy and poor implementation. Applying internal organizational modes of operation, such as hierarchical authority; command-and-control; top-down, one-way communications; or internal functions and processes, can yield dismal results if used to address a wicked problem. Best practice is for managers to determine whether a wicked problem exists by conceptualizing the problem broadly, using a focus that is internal and external to the organization, and to decide on the proper strategic response, transition between the internal organization and the external networked arrangement, and manage collaboratively.

Discussion Questions

1. Define and discuss conceptualization. How can managers conceptualize from both an internal and an external perspective?

2. Identify and discuss some of the negative consequences that can occur when a manager fails to conceptualize a problem.

3. What are wicked challenges? What differentiates a wicked challenge from the normal challenges that public managers face? Give examples of some wicked problems.

4. Identify and discuss the collaborative management skills that a manager needs to master to be successful. Why is collaboration important when a manager has to handle a wicked problem?

Notes

1. Michael Stahl, "Promoting Problem-Based Public Management," *PA Times* (May 2009): 32.
2. Trevor L. Brown and Matthew Potoski, "Transaction Costs and Institutional Explanations for Government Service Production Decisions," *Journal of Public Administration Research and Theory* 13 (2003): 441.
3. Horst W.J. Rittel and Melvin Webber, "Dilemmas in a General Theory of Planning," *Policy Sciences* 4 (1973): 155.
4. Jean-Marie Buijs, "Understanding the Connective Capacity of Program Management in Complex Governance Processes from a Self-Organization Perspective" (paper presented at the American Society for Public Administration Annual Conference, Miami, FL, 2009).
5. Christopher E. Claunch, Presentation to Texas City Management Association regional meeting, West University Place, TX, 2009.
6. Michael McGuire, "Managing Networks: Propositions on What Managers Do and Why They Do It," *Public Administration Review* 62 (2002): 599.
7. Chester C. Cotton, "Marginality—A Neglected Dimension in the Design of Work," *The Academy of Management Review* 2 (1977): 133; W.W. Liddell, "Marginality and Integrative Decisions," *The Academy of Management Journal* 16 (1973): 154; H. O. Pruden and B. J. Stark, "Marginality Associated with Interorganizational Linking Process, Productivity, and Satisfaction," *The Academy of Management Journal* 14 (1971): 145.
8. Robert Agranoff and Michael McGuire, *Collaborative Public Management: New Strategies for Local Government* (Washington, D.C.: Georgetown University Press, 2003).
9. Myrna P. Mandell, "The Impact of Collaborative Efforts: Changing the Face of Public Policy Through Networks and Network Structures," *Policy Studies Review* 16 (1999): 4; Laurence J. O'Toole Jr., "Treating Networks Seriously: Practical and Research-Based Agendas in Public Administration," *Public Administration Review* 57 (1997): 45.
10. Michael McGuire, "Collaborative Public Management: Assessing What We Know and How We Know It," *Public Administration Review* 66 (2006): 33.

CHAPTER 2 ─────────────────────────

Planning and Managing Core Mission Functions in San Diego County, California

Jackie Werth and Dale R. Fleming

The key to success in strategic planning is not so much how the planning is done, but how the planning progresses from strategic thinking to strategic action, from paper to practice. One of the primary purposes of local government is to make real what federal and state governments envision and mandate. In today's complex, dynamic public sector, it is by necessity and for the benefit of local residents that local governments plan proactively to ensure that what is implemented works and brings maximum value to the citizenry. This chapter describes the infrastructure of San Diego County, California, that makes conversion of strategy to reality possible. We then describe how this works within the county's Health and Human Services Agency (HHSA) and in several major HHSA initiatives.

The Discipline of a General Management System

In the mid-1990s, San Diego County was near bankruptcy. The state had raided local revenues, and the county was facing increasing demands for services from citizens and had invested in some costly ventures, most notably a money-losing waste-to-energy facility.

Fortunately, a chief administrative officer and his deputy, both executives with private sector experience, helped turn the county's finances around by organizing the county along business-model lines, selling the losing landfill venture, launching a managed competition for the provision of selected services, and introducing a new framework for operations, the General Management System (GMS), that is still in use today. Continuity in leadership on both the board of supervisors and in county government, unusual for local government, allowed the GMS to take hold and mature. It now underpins a strong five-part planning and management system (see Figure 2-1).

Today, the county has three high-level initiatives (Kids, Environment, and Safe and Livable Communities) that represent priorities the public cares about and to which all departments contribute. A number of *required disciplines* capture competencies essential to fulfilling these initiatives— such as fiscal stability; a skilled, adaptable, and diverse workforce; and customer satisfaction. These initiatives and disciplines are made real or operational through a budget, departmental operational plans, and executive performance goals. Employee recognition and rewards are also aligned to high-level strategy. More powerful still is the cooperative approach departments take in the resource allocation process, particularly in difficult economic times, by sharing budget dollars and staff resources and aligning activities to advance strategic goals.

Figure 2-1: The Five-Part GMS Cycle

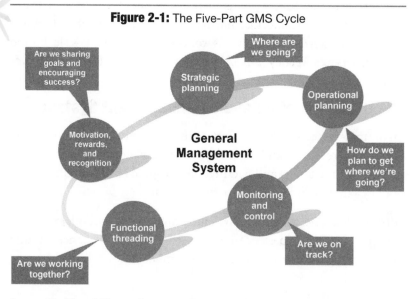

Source: Health and Human Services Agency, San Diego County

A Complex Health and Human Services Agency Grapples with Strategic Alignment

But none of this has come easily. It has taken time to develop this simple, powerful, and mature planning and management system. The challenges are best illustrated by the experiences of HHSA and two recent and inter-related initiatives—a food stamps program and a reengineering of the public welfare eligibility system.

The county embarked upon a major redesign of its health and human services at about the same time it adopted its business model (mid-1990s). Five separate departments—health services, the area agency on aging, public administrator/public guardian, social services, and a local commission for children, youth, and families—were combined under a single executive to create a mega- or super-agency. A wide range of health and social services were to be delivered out of six regions, each with its own regional general manager (see Figure 2-2). The idea was to facilitate the tailoring of services to meet community needs, enhance prevention efforts, and emphasize service integration to support the self-sufficiency of end-users and better health outcomes.

Figure 2-2: Health and Human Services Agency Regions

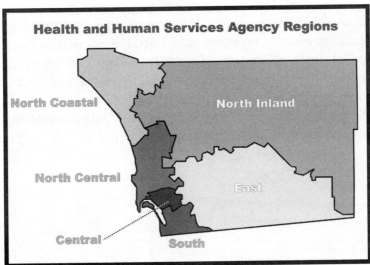

Source: Health and Human Services Agency, San Diego County

It was by necessity that HHSA managed strategically—realigning a wide range of disparate planning and delivery systems to more efficaciously address what ultimately were common or overlapping programmatic requirements. Given its complexity and its mandate to provide better services for the community without growing in size, such a strategic realignment on the part of the county was a logical choice. After numerous attempts at strategic planning, drawing upon various planning methodologies, a simple hybrid approach was adopted. Based on a multitude of planning goals and more than 700 performance measures, HHSA developed, and still uses, a one-page strategy agenda. Created in 2005, the strategy agenda sorts all agency programs and activities into priority service areas, six mission-critical services, and 17 result indicators. Its beauty is in its simplicity. It has also proven to be a good communication tool. Internally, staff members can see their roles and responsibilities; externally, community members can see that the agency is working toward goals they care about.

The HHSA executive team came up with the framework (vision, mission, priority service areas, and mission-critical services). Significantly, feedback from 17 citizen advisory committees informed the framework. As part of a budget exercise in fiscal year 2003–04, these citizen committees prioritized services, helping executives learn which ones were most essential and valued. Then, focus groups of managers and program experts articulated the measures that would indicate the agency's progress toward its goals. For example, multiple regions and divisions can show that they contribute to the mission-critical goal of *access*: Senior service programs link older adults to mental health services, the mental health services division helps ensure adolescents receive outpatient care, and outreach and eligibility staff across multiple programs enroll eligible children and families in health insurance programs (see Figure 2-3).

Figure 2-3: Measuring Performance toward a Mission-Critical Goal

Goal: Assisting at-risk and vulnerable people to be safe, healthy, and self-sufficient, and protecting the public's health

Access: Enrollment in medical, dental, and behavioral health services

- % increase in older adults receiving mental health services
- % increase in transition-age youth receiving mental health outpatient services
- % net enrollment gain of children in Medi-Cal and Healthy Families

Source: Health and Human Services Agency, San Diego County

No fix is complete, however. Challenges persist. One of the most vexing is managing effectively as a matrix organization (see Figure 2-4). There are horizontal and vertical lines of authority, making clarity in direction and robust communication imperative. The advantages of a matrixed organization include unlimited potential for leveraging resources and creative approaches to advance shared results—for example, tapping scarce expertise and assets across organization boundaries that might otherwise not be available in a smaller, stove-piped arrangement. Nevertheless, there may also be confusion regarding who leads, who should contribute, and what the expectations are. This is a continuing struggle.

But as the agency matures, communication channels have deepened, and the agency has begun to build a track record of success through innovation and cooperation. HHSA regularly holds *cross-threaded meetings*, at which all regions and divisions are represented, at all levels of the organization. When performance goals are established each year, regions and divisions are expected to identify how they will support each other. Special priority initiatives engage everyone.

Figure 2-4: Managing a Matrix Organization

No Choice but to Manage Strategically

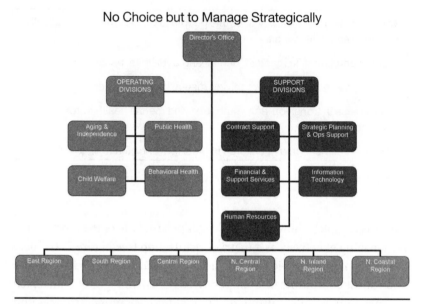

Source: Health and Human Services Agency, San Diego County

Theory in Practice

At HHSA, there is a shared sense of responsibility for achieving results, thanks to this simple strategy agenda framework and the GMS discipline undergirding it. Two key initiatives illustrate how this has worked in practical terms.

All Hands Engaged in Priority Food Stamps Initiative

As the number of San Diego County families in economic distress grew, the county's board of supervisors demanded that staff enroll more eligible households in the county's food stamps program. Many potentially eligible families in the county were not participating in the program because they were unaware that they qualified for it or were dissuaded by the stigma associated with the program or its complex eligibility process.

The original intent of the food stamps program, when it was first piloted in 1939, was to distribute surplus farm-grown goods to low-income families. Over time, the program had been siloed as a public welfare initiative, contributing to its stigma.

To revamp the program, the HHSA director called an all-day, all-hands meeting. Staff from across HHSA and a few from other county departments were assigned to teams to brainstorm strategies, with the goal of promoting nutrition among low-income families while streamlining eligibility and preserving program integrity.

What came of the all-hands meeting? The public health officer saw an opportunity to address poor eating habits and counter obesity, a major problem in San Diego just as it is in the rest of the country. The directors of the mental health and alcohol and drug services departments noted the importance of healthy eating to the recovery of their clients. The Farm Bureau recognized a business opportunity for local growers and farmers' markets. The board of supervisors developed and accepted a comprehensive Nutrition Security Plan and set a challenging goal for the agency: to increase enrollment of children and seniors in the food stamps program by 50,000 within three years.

The beauty of aligning the participating departments through the GMS is that the same goals appear in the executive performance plans of all regions and divisions that play a part. Because of HHSA's strategic alignment, it was able to market the food stamps program as both a public health initiative and a self-sufficiency program. This approach was not only innovative, but also allowed the program to return to its roots as a vehicle for promoting healthy eating and helping local agriculture by encouraging the purchase of local fruits and vegetables.

Now, outreach practices borrowed from public health are being used to reach clients. All clients, regardless of where they enter HHSA's system, are told how to enroll in the program and are offered nutrition education whenever possible. Another county department is helping by equipping local farmers' markets so they can accept electronic benefit transfer of food stamp dollars.

Reengineering the Eligibility System

A redesign of local business processes was integral to enhancing access to the food stamps program. There was a growing recognition that the eligibility system for all county public assistance programs—Medi-Cal, food stamps, CalWORKs—could not keep pace with future demands. But what actually sparked the business process review (BPR) of eligibility were data showing that San Diego was among the lowest-ranked counties in terms of case-processing productivity. Clearly, there were opportunities for improvement. Looking down the road, the county had to do better; service expectations were only going to increase, while staff levels would, at best, stay the same. The performance gap had to be closed. Midway through this redesign effort, the economy tanked, making the BPR an absolute imperative.

This ambitious eligibility BPR was intended to streamline business processes and make them more efficient. Virtually everyone at HHSA was enlisted or engaged in the BPR in some way. The geographic regions embarked on a series of mini-pilots and projects in individual Family Resource Centers (FRCs) to explore new ways of doing business. This included training workers to process requirements of multiple programs to achieve efficiencies, an effort led by the South Region. The Central Region took the lead on the technology efforts by imaging case records and converting all case information into electronic files. Strategic Planning and Operational Support, HHSA's policy division, retooled internal support activities, including application support provided to the CalWIN system, the eligibility database system HHSA has been using since June 2006. Related training was expanded and revamped, which required HHSA's human resources division to coordinate closely with the regions so that staff would be trained to meet the demands of a new operating environment.

The changes have been truly transformational. Personnel have begun to use a task-based, same-day intake model. All FRCs are now transitioning to a paperless case management system. More and more staff will be trained in multiple programs. A new ACCESS customer service center has opened to help customers apply for assistance, update their case information, make appointments, and obtain other services. In this way, customers can avoid unnecessary trips to the FRCs, and requiring that a new organizational culture be reinforced both internally and externally—through training and changes in routine. Workers need to see clients as customers and to treat all customers responsively and respectfully. The work environment must promote learning and receptiveness to new ways of doing business.

The BPR effort is significant because it was initiated at the local level, not by the state, and the new processes were designed in partnership between labor and management. The changes made to the eligibility system that had been used for 30 years were arguably of the "shock and awe" variety. HHSA borrowed from the private sector an emphasis on customer service, just-in-time manufacturing, task-based processing, and cross-training, among other practices. (Here, task-based processing means that cases are broken into tasks and more people touch every individual case, reducing the likelihood that any one case will be lost, backlogged, or handled incorrectly.) At the same time, best practices of the public sector were maintained—namely, transparency and accountability to staff, stakeholders, and the public—throughout the redesign. Continuous measurement and progress reporting were absolute tenets of the project.

The eligibility BPR sparked fears, just as it inspired excitement. For some workers, the redesign was like facing the abyss; they were leaving behind everything they knew. Another challenge was getting staff to think beyond themselves and their own workloads, beyond even their FRCs or regions. While the old culture had allowed, perhaps even encouraged, variations in practice between regions, the BPR requires consistent practices and adherence to processes proven to be most efficient. Staff also had to learn that the system takes precedence and that everyone's role is to optimize the productivity of the entire system.

The new model passed its first test. As more families sought help in a tough economy, four FRCs were struggling to keep up with the caseloads. Four other high-performing FRCs stepped up—each adopted one of the other four offices. A new system capability, virtual caseloads, enabled cases to be shifted to other offices without having to move staff, improving the efficiency of the entire system. In essence, this is *surge capacity*—the ability to direct work from one location to another in order to equalize the workload and get a better result—at work. This new capability has tremendous potential, particularly in times of emergency, such as when firestorms devastated the county in 2007. In the future, FRCs in affected areas will be able to redirect or "outsource" the many food stamp applications submitted by families dislocated by fires. Other FRCs will process them remotely.

Once again, GMS discipline was exercised throughout the eligibility BPR. Project milestones became part of executive performance plans and region and division business plans. The HHSA team formulated project metrics at the outset, and these results continue to be monitored to assess progress on key dimensions—customer, process or internal, financial, and human resources. These include measures of progress in training of staff in multiple programs, in cases being imaged, and in case-processing times. Project status reporting should happen early and often, even at the highest levels; the county executive team is given in-depth briefings every quarter.

The Third Dimension: Engaging Citizens and Stakeholders

Engaging citizens is one of the most daunting and difficult aspects of local government reform efforts. Local governments often face distrust from the community regarding redesign or reform efforts, particularly when stakeholders are not convinced that these reforms are about anything other than saving money. This is why project goals and messages must be carefully articulated with the client in mind and with a genuine view of clients as customers.

HHSA has 17 citizen advisory boards composed of stakeholders, some of whom are also subject matter experts, who meet regularly to advise the agency on its initiatives and direction. These citizen advisory boards were consulted and gave HHSA vitally important feedback when the agency strategy agenda, the food stamp initiative, and the eligibility BPR were designed.

It can be far more difficult to directly engage community advocates in systems change. Much can be learned from advocates about client needs and barriers they face in accessing services, but advocates believe their primary responsibility is to serve as the voice of clients and their needs. They can be suspicious of change efforts. For example, advocates wanted the food stamps program to be expanded quickly and broadly throughout the community. These advocates were not as interested in reforming the system.

GMS 2.0

Change doesn't rest. In fact, change begets more change. Recognizing this, county leadership has taken the GMS to the next level. The GMS framework that undergirds all of the agency's initiatives and that has established the guideposts for translating vision and strategy into reality has been given a new name in San Diego County—GMS 2.0. GMS 2.0 calls for the same discipline but a more urgent sense of the need to be aware of and prepare for change. Most important, GMS 2.0 calls upon all county employees, regardless of department or position, to look for new and better ways to get things done. Accordingly, the county is heavily promoting the idea of the "knowledge" worker, who is constantly learning and adapting, through desktop trainings, guided discussions between supervisors and staff, and a website offering articles and a variety of other resources.

As the pace of change quickens, local governments cannot wait for federal or state solutions. Nor are federal and state solutions forthcoming in today's environment, given the limited capacities, resources, and influence of federal and state governments. The local government must act as a strategic player, translating strategic thinking into strategic action, in addition to anticipating and formulating new strategic directions. Locals will make it happen, while being poised for rapid and relentless waves of change.

Discussion Questions

1. What are the five major elements of San Diego County's GMS and how do they serve to achieve priority outcomes?

2. How has this discipline proven successful in the county's Food Stamps initiative?

3. How has it worked in re-engineering the county's public welfare eligibility system?

4. How has HHSA met the challenge of managing in a matrix organization? What strategic benefits has the county reaped from this approach?

5. How has HHSA engaged citizens in these initiatives? How has this process benefited the county strategically?

CHAPTER 3

Planning and Resource Decision-Making at the Federal Level

Tim E. Winchell, Sr.

Over the last 35 years, the American private sector has increasingly moved away from the classic command-and-control, hierarchical, top-down decision-making structures and cultures characteristic of the postwar era. Organizations have become more flexible, team-based, and capable of strategically responding to rapidly emerging market opportunities and the vicissitudes of global economics. The federal government, particularly in the last 20 years, has also put increased emphasis on strategic planning, team-based problem-solving, and customer-focused program assessment.

Nonetheless, classic command-and-control structures remain in place in many agencies. While internal agency cultures vary markedly, management behaviors relative to the planning and resource allocation processes are surprisingly consistent and have changed little over decades. This chapter identifies the structural and regulatory bases for these behaviors and provides recommendations for enhancing federal productivity.

The Conundrum of Measuring Public Sector Productivity

When total quality management principles are applied, a strong case can be made that the inputs/outputs definition of productivity used by the U.S. Bureau of Labor Statistics (BLS) is sufficient to measure productivity in the private sector, the logic being that creating quality at the point of origin reduces rework and inspection costs (inputs), while raising customer satisfaction and demand rates (outputs)—a win-win for both producers and consumers. The outcome of consistently providing quality, sought-after products and services is profit margins that sustain the company and ensure its long-term growth and viability.

In the public sector, a consistent pattern of profits is typically not the desired outcome for a program. Outcomes are often outlined in legislation as broadly based national security, health, international affairs, or social policies that reflect political priorities that may not be well defined. Measuring program performance in public environments requires that outcomes be an integral part of the productivity measurement equation. The work of Walter Balk in the 1970s and 1980s on public-sector productivity measurement and the more recent discussion by Martin Cole and Greg Parston in *Unlocking Public Value* emphasize the difficulty of measuring outcomes in assessing program effectiveness in public environments.

Cited as an example in various texts, including Cole and Parston's, is the issue of crime rates. When submitting a budget request for additional police officers, a police chief might attribute a reduction in crime to a proportional increase in the number of patrols in an area. If more patrols (outputs) equal lower crime (outcomes), then hiring more police (inputs) will continue to improve outcomes. But is this necessarily the best way to lower crime and use taxpayer dollars? What role might a strong economy have had? An improved education system, harsher sentencing laws, and declining birthrates in the area? Would crime in the long term be lowered more by establishing a sustainable environment with a strong economy and well-educated citizenry? We can see that it is difficult to establish a hypothesis that specific outputs are the cause of a specific outcome when assessing productivity in areas of public policy.

That is not to say that outputs that include quality assessments cannot be measured against costs relatively easily in some federal operational environments. Department of Defense (DoD) facilities involved with armaments manufacturing or repair of ships or airplanes have well-established metrics and accounting tools for measuring the relative productivity of operations in terms of production rates, production quality, and cost, much like their private-sector counterparts. Many federal agencies produce products or provide services (such as advice and guidance directly to customers) that can be assessed separately from the impact these outputs may have on the larger outcome issues, such as the adequacy of the national defense or the social safety net. The measurement of outputs becomes particularly difficult in areas such as research, foreign affairs, and national security, in which a significant portion of the work involves applying intellectual capital to address broad outcomes directly, rather than attempting to meet predefined repetitive production schedules.

Regardless of the difficulty or the context, measuring federal operational performance is an imperative increasingly emphasized over the last two decades. Examples include Vice President Al Gore's National Performance Review (NPR) in the 1990s, passage of the Government Performance and Results Act (GPRA) in 1993, President George W. Bush's 2001 President's Management Agenda (PMA), and various agency-level risk assessment programs with requirements to report to the U.S. Office of Management and Budget (OMB), consistent with a 1995 OMB memorandum outlining risk analysis principles.

Open and Closed Organizations

Thirty years ago, informal surveys of my adult, working professional students typically found little difference in public- and private-sector organizational structures or the reporting relationships between federal, state, and local government employees and those in the private sector. Tom Burns and G.M. Stalker's description of *closed model organizations*, characterized by routine tasks occurring in stable conditions; task specialization; an emphasis on means over ends; conflict adjudicated from the top; hierarchy, with its superior/subordinate relationships; and other features was evident regardless of employer. *Open model organizations*, which are fluid, results-oriented, and team-based; emphasize free-flowing vertical and lateral communications; and have the ability to rapidly assemble teams of appropriate experts from throughout the organization, were limited primarily to academic and research environments.

Today when I survey, students from the private sector routinely say the open model is more characteristic of their work environment than the closed. Students working for government, particularly the federal government, characterize their environments as more closed model.

This is not to say that the federal government is less committed to teamwork. Teamwork has been particularly emphasized since the early 1990s when, for a time, real momentum developed throughout the federal government to adopt the strategic planning, process simplification, and team-based problem-solving methods of the total quality movement. While exceptions exist, teams in federal environments are typically of the *process action team* variety: assembled to enable the employees working in the process to address specific problems identified by management relative to process flow, customer support, or quality. The rapid movement of experts among teams—often as part of multiple teams working concurrently—to focus on emerging client priorities is characteristic of large consulting firms. This was and is not the norm in federal agencies.

The reality is that management practices between the private and public sectors have diverged significantly over the last decades in response to specific environmental priorities. Private-sector migration to flexible, team-based structures is a response to extremely diverse, rapidly changing consumer markets in which output/input metrics adequately measure productivity against companies' consistent long-term outcome requirement: profitability. Federal agencies have become increasingly sensitive to the need for effective performance measurement, with an emphasis on oversight and reporting through defined strategic plans and performance metrics necessitated, in part, by the need to integrate outcome parameters into the productivity equation. Maintenance of largely command-and-control structures with well-defined and long-established specialized hierarchies remains the best way to monitor the cost-effectiveness of federal operations and to allocate congressionally mandated financial and human resources, while remaining aligned with political and policy priorities.

Understanding Management Behavior in Federal Environments

Federal managers play by the rules. The corruption endemic in many foreign governments is virtually unheard of among federal managers. While reasonable risk-taking to enhance the accomplishment of mission is tolerated within legal parameters, any misuse of government funds or resources for personal benefit is dealt with harshly.

Federal managers almost universally believe the products and services they provide positively contribute to the well-being of the United States and its residents and allies. They take great pride in delivering quality to those they service. They operate within a set of prescribed rules relative to planning and resource allocation. They understand the processes for requesting and tracking resources and how best to present their case to secure the resources necessary to maintain the health of their programs. They know that successful program execution requires pragmatic resource management.

Federal managers often make decisions knowing that there are few current metrics available to measure actual workload and project accurate staffing requirements to meet the defined strategic objectives. Rapidly changing mission requirements, the pace of technological change, and the imperative to minimize overhead costs have made it difficult for many agencies to devote the resources necessary to develop and identify accurate and current workload data and align meaningful, realistic staffing standards and budgets with strategic objectives.

Shifting political priorities further complicate the process when funding is augmented or cut based upon political criteria and not past performance. While identifying resource requirements is difficult enough in complex operational settings such as shipyards, squadrons, and check-processing centers, it becomes particularly problematic in areas where work involves the application of intellectual capital. For all the recent emphasis on performance measurement, establishing budgets and staffing controls is rarely a surgically precise exercise.

Committed to program excellence and aware of the need for additional resources to maximize program performance, managers respond to the annual, supplemental, and unfunded requirements budget calls by documenting their case. They are also aware that the lack of metrics that clearly establish minimal budget and staffing requirements in defined program areas will likely result in agencywide, horizontal "fair share" downsizing cuts during lean times. When those cuts come, those already operating at maximum capacity to accomplish their most minimally defined missions will appear to be the most inefficient managers, while those who have expanded their mission and resources to include services beyond the minimum will be able to continue meeting their minimum objectives after they absorb their fair share cuts. Charles Levine referred to this as the *efficiency paradox*. Managers also realize that vertical cuts, where entire programs are eliminated in lieu of everyone "sharing the pain," are highly unlikely, either because the programs are mandated by statute or because they have advocates who will fight at the political level to continue them.

Today's Federal Reality

Complicating the allocation of resources, leadership turns over rapidly in federal environments. Military and United States Foreign Service officers typically rotate every two to three years. Political appointees average even shorter tenures. The retirement tsunami of the last few years has also contributed. Yet regardless of the tenure of leaders, top-down resource controls, an emphasis on internal process integrity driven by congressional and OMB oversight, and constantly changing information technology mandate that real change must be supported and initiated by senior management with a goal of embedding the change philosophy in all levels of the agency. What is needed is a change model compatible with today's federal reality.

Organizational development (OD) training and team-building methods have been in use in many federal agencies for years. Many federal managers consider team-building and other behavioral training of the OD variety to be harmless feel-good or "touchy-feely" tactics that are not easily incorporated into their daily reality. Comprehensive, bottom-up, culture-driven change, as originally posited by Wendell L. French and Cecil H. Bell, Jr., in their classic *Organizational Development*, has been no more successful in the federal government than in the private sector.

Within a few years of gaining momentum in the federal government in the early 1990s, the total quality management (TQM) movement lost steam, largely relegated to the same closet as earlier major program initiatives such as governmentwide implementation of DoD's program-planning-budgeting system (PPBS) in the 1960s and 1970s, President Jimmy Carter's zero-based budgeting in the 1970s, and more targeted efforts to incorporate the *In Search of Excellence* principles recommended by Thomas J. Peters and Robert H. Waterman, Jr., in the early 1980s.

This was indeed unfortunate, because the TQM movement's emphasis on strategic planning and top-down, process-driven change through well-trained and clearly focused process-action teams was compatible with closed-model federal reality and congressionally mandated planning and program assessment and was distinctly different from the OD change model with which it was regularly confused.

The nature of top-down policymaking and the resource allocation process mandates that today's federal managers require a coherent infrastructure of defined strategic objectives aligned to a rational resource allocation process, in which program execution, to the extent reasonably possible, applies measurement metrics that assess both outputs and outcomes.

Where Do We Go from Here?

So how can the new Obama administration maximize performance in today's federal government environment? Here are some pointers the U.S. Office of Management and Budget and other departmental management officials might want to consider:

1. **Do not reinvent the wheel.** Considerable time and effort has been expended over the last 20 years to develop logical performance

measurement tools. Use what works within the context of a closed-model, resource-driven reality.

2. **Accept the closed-model reality.** Profit is not an outcome of most federal programs. The cost-effectiveness of program execution is often in the eyes of the beholder and is hardly transparent. Effective resource management requires strong position management programs that, to the extent possible, rationally align strategic objectives to optimal organizational structures, strategic human resources planning programs to address turnover, and reasonable workload metrics. Whereas private-sector managers tend to be keenly aware of their labor costs and the impact these have on profits, in federal environments managers below the most senior levels typically have little knowledge of how resources are allocated and revert to the squeaky-wheel approach when defending their resource requests.

In federal agencies, real analysis of workload and identification of optimal organizational structures to support strategic program execution ranges from sophisticated, using a variety of metrics, to (in many cases) virtually nonexistent, ad hoc in response to emerging realities, and typically limited to mandatory submissions as part of budget and full-time equivalency (FTE, representing staff work-year authorizations) requests. Unless resource analysis tools and programs aligned to execute strategic objectives are established, adequately funded, and monitored, true outcomes-based productivity measurement is impossible, given the complexity of federal operations.

3. **Create cultures that support change.** Investing in people to enhance their skill in identifying process improvements to improve output/input performance ratios is a first step toward positive change. Even employees responsible for producing intellectual capital (vs. specific products or services) are always aware of internal communications problems and process redundancies. The greatest demotivator found in most federal agencies is convoluted and incoherent processes that do not provide the necessary information

to efficiently accomplish the work but do overwhelm staff with unneeded, unwanted communications. And untold productivity is lost when employees are required to manually bridge the data gap among software applications that cannot talk with each other.

Resurfacing the TQM emphasis on program analysis through process action teams working toward well-defined process improvement goals is particularly important. Recognition incentives should be coupled with transparency in how these productivity enhancements will impact career stability and minimize resistance.

4. **Define leadership in terms of top-down reality.** Management training and incentive programs must be clearly aligned with accomplishment of strategic objectives, while consistently improving outcomes-based productivity (even if the outcomes are broken down into individual output metrics). This has already been happening in federal agencies, and it must be continuously supported and increasingly linked to emerging position management assessment criteria. Particular emphasis should be placed on minimizing fair-share resource-reduction practices and using workload metrics as the basis for more precisely realigning resource priorities. When such measures are in place, senior managers can better reward those subordinate managers who most cost-effectively manage their resources and discourage the "give me more" mentality that has long been reinforced under the efficiency paradox.

The foundation has been laid to establish true performance management cultures aligned to the federal closed-model reality. With appropriate training and incentives, federal leaders can continue to successfully enhance performance, in alignment with emerging administration priorities.

Discussion Questions

1. How does measuring outcomes in the public sector differ from the private sector's bottom-line approach?

2. What is the efficiency paradox, and how does this Catch-22 create winners and losers when operating budgets are reduced?

3. What actions will have the greatest impact on maximizing performance in today's federal government environment?

4. What do you think the author means by "clearly align[ing]... management training and incentive programs [with] accomplishment of strategic objectives?"

Recommended Resources

Balk, Walter L. *Improving Government Productivity: Some Policy Perspectives.* Beverly Hills, CA: Sage Publications, 1975.

Burns, Tom, and G. M. Stalker. *The Management of Innovation.* London: Tavistock, 1961.

Cole, Martin, and Greg Parston. *Unlocking Public Value.* Hoboken, NJ: Wiley, 2006.

Executive Office of the President and the U.S. Office of Management and Budget. *The President's Management Agenda* (Washington, D.C., 2001). http://www.whitehouse.gov/omb/budget/fy2002/mgmt.pdf (accessed November 24, 2009).

French, Wendell L., and Cecil H. Bell, Jr. *Organizational Development: Behavioral Science Interventions for Organization Improvement.* Englewood Cliffs, NJ: Prentice-Hall, 1973.

Levine, Charles. "More on Cutback Management: Hard Questions for Hard Times," *Public Management Forum* 39 (March/April 1979): 179–183.

Peters, Thomas J., and Robert H. Waterman, Jr. *In Search of Excellence: Lessons from America's Best-Run Companies.* New York: Harper and Row, 1982.

PART 2

Strategic Budget and Financial Management

CHAPTER 4

Managing Risk in the Federal Fiscal Environment

Nancy Fagenson Potok and Aaron B. Corbett

Do you know what your risk is of not being able to accomplish your agency's mission? If you are like many of today's government managers, you started thinking about risk in a serious way after September 11, 2001. During the past eight years, you have worked to improve awareness among your employees about IT security. You have increased physical security at your location and, if you are a federal manager, you have been implementing Homeland Security Presidential Directive 12, known familiarly as HSPD12, which requires identity verification, background checks, and the collection of biometric information for the people who get badges to enter your buildings. If you are a federal financial manager, you also have been busy for the last 15 years or so making sure that you are in compliance with the Chief Financial Officers Act of 1990, the Government Performance and Review Act of 1993, and the Government Management and Reform Act of 1994. And if you haven't already developed a Continuity of Operations Plan, or COOP, for your agency, you are surely about to do it. But in spite of all the time and resources you have devoted to compliance, if you are like most of your colleagues, when you are tossing and turning at 2:00 a.m., chances are high that you are worrying about something that is putting your agency at risk of failure.

Risk Management

We all know that risks cannot be completely eliminated. But they can be managed. And as a manager, it is up to you to make the strategic and tactical decisions on how your organization's risks will be treated. That is, what level of risk can you accept? What risks can be deferred, what risks can be reduced, and what risks can be transferred, avoided, or controlled? Undertaking the process of identifying, analyzing, measuring, and controlling risks within your own standards of acceptability is what risk management is all about.

Risk management generally consists of three phases:

- Identification
- Measurement
- Management.

Identification

Identification of risk means understanding what your risks are and their sources, including how various risks interact with each other. This requires an assessment of the external environment and internal processes and procedures. Of course, if you are in a government agency, you probably have help with this from your inspector general, outside auditors, the U.S. Government Accountability Office (GAO) or its state government equivalent, and your legislative oversight bodies. Additionally, you and your management team may have brought in your own consultants to help with this assessment.

Measurement

Measurement of risk can be accomplished using a variety of approaches. But all methods involve collecting and maintaining appropriate data. This can get to be quite an expensive activity, so it is always important to make sure that the costs of the data collection are proportional to the level of risk you are managing. Measuring and categorizing risks allows you to determine whether risks are major or minor, and following that, the level of resources you want to devote to managing the identified risks. Clearly, you want to focus first on the risks that you have deemed a high priority and that you can manage. At the opposite end are risks that are a low priority and beyond your control to manage.

Management

Management of risk is not for the faint of heart. That is, an organization's management must make a commitment and sustained effort to develop a risk management culture. Risk management can be passive or active; regardless, it starts with policy development and assignment of responsibilities throughout the organization.

Generally, top management will develop the policies and determine the acceptable levels of risk for the organization. These policies and procedures will have to conform to any standards established by outside oversight and audit agencies, such as the U.S. Office of Management and Budget (OMB) and GAO. In addition, the program managers in your agency must find ways to accomplish their mission while still conforming to the agency's risk management policies and procedures. Finally, a staff function is needed for collecting and analyzing data to track risk and report to management. Agency managers frequently struggle to determine the level of authority for this non-line management cadre. Giving staff personnel too much authority can lead to a perceived burden on program managers; insufficient authority will hamper the staff's ability to collect and interpret accurate data. To the extent that data can be collected automatically and analyzed electronically, some of these tensions may be alleviated, if not eliminated.

Risk Management in the National Security Arena

Even as most governmental agencies have become fairly adept at financial risk management over the past 15 years, other agencies have been working across their traditional organizational boundaries to enhance risk management in the national security arena. The National Infrastructure Advisory Council provides the president with advice on security of critical infrastructure through the secretary of Homeland Security. A 2005 report from the Council on Risk Management[1] concluded that effective risk management methods share common attributes. Among these are:

- **A mature understanding of failure mechanisms and failure indicators.** In studying the *Challenger* space shuttle disaster, among others, the Council discovered that the National Aeronautics and Space Administration's own assessment found, through a more mature risk analysis of the heat shield tiles, that 15 percent of the tiles represented 85 percent of the heat shield risk. Artificial time constraints compromised work on the tiles. When we couple actuarial data with such human factors, we realize that a more mature understanding of the failure mechanisms would have allowed greater focus on the highest-risk parts of the heat shield.

- **Effective use of data, including its conversion to actionable information.** The Council also looked at the 9/11 Commission Report and noted that a key risk management failure was a failure to integrate data in an efficient and reliable manner, especially across the intelligence community. Rapid synthesis of information to help risk managers identify potential risks and potential means of managing the outcomes is a function of having standardized methods and the capability to deliver actionable reports.

- **Institution of a risk management culture across all levels of the organization, with a single point of accountability for risk management (e.g., a risk management officer).** The inclusion of oversight functions creates a necessary bridge between risk assessment and risk management activities. The Council's second and third overall recommendations include the creation of a departmental chief risk officer and central oversight body to accomplish what private companies do through their boards of directors.

- **Training to lessen technical and procedural human error.** The *Challenger* disaster also revealed that lower wages led to high turnover among key construction personnel and a workforce with limited expertise. A more mature mechanism includes ongoing training.

- **A strong business case for investments in risk management.** Developing a culture of risk management across an agency and prioritizing it in the budget is a practice the public sector can take from private-sector firms successful in risk management.

The National Infrastructure Advisory Council's overall recommendation was for the government to continue its focus on risk management. With regard to the effective risk management methods listed above, it made three primary recommendations:

1. Create and standardize risk management methodologies and mechanisms across the government.

2. Establish a risk management leadership function within departments, bureaus, or agencies.

3. Establish a risk management oversight function.

Private-Sector Perspectives

A 2007 survey by The Economist Intelligence Unit[2] of 238 private-sector executives found that while traditional aspects of risk management, including financial and market risk, remain fundamental, reputational and human capital risks are becoming increasingly important. Fewer than half of the executives surveyed thought that their organizations were effectively managing physical security, terrorism, reputational, natural hazard, human capital, and climate change risk. Some of the barriers to effective risk management identified by these executives were lack of clarity in lines of responsibility for risk management; lack of resources and time; the difficulty of identifying and assessing emerging risks; and the threat from unknown, unforeseeable risks.

These views from the private sector are equally relevant in the public sector. Of particular note was the strongly held belief that, although support from top management was important, the key determinant of success in managing risk was a strong culture and awareness of risk throughout the organization. But how effective is creating a widespread awareness of risk unless you have the ability to accurately convert data into accurate, actionable information in a timely way? In our plugged-in world, our problems often stem from being awash in too much information, with no time to sort through it and decide how to respond. So we take shortcuts, gravitate toward information that reinforces what we think we already know, and quickly discard information that seems irrelevant. And that is how major mistakes are made.

These lessons are well known to the national intelligence community, which is populated by analysts who are trained to systematically sift through large volumes of information with strategic, operational, or tactical importance to determine the probability of future actions in specific situations. Intelligence analysis helps reduce the ambiguity of ambiguous situations. It consists of a combination of techniques designed to overcome natural cognitive biases, which are a function of the analyst's own personality and the organizational culture.

Common Errors in Risk Management

The national intelligence community has identified several common errors made by analysts that lead to poor analysis and, at worst, major intelligence failures. Key among these errors is the *analytical mindset*— that is, the tendency to jump to conclusions prematurely or to be unduly swayed by a group's mindset, which becomes increasingly likely under time pressures. Some of the most common cognitive failures include:

- *Mirror imaging,* or assuming that someone else's mindset is like your own

- *Idea fixation,* or only looking for evidence that supports a preformed hypothesis (this is especially common when in a hurry)

- *Inappropriate analogies,* which are made when there is insufficient knowledge about the context in which information exists or activities are occurring

- *Stovepiping,* or the functional separation that occurs when various parts of an organization do not share information

- *Rational-actor hypothesis*, which ascribes "rational" behavior to the other side, but with the definition of rationality coming from one's own culture

- *Proportionality bias,* or assuming that priorities are the same between different cultures—e.g., that small things are small in every culture

- *Deception,* or misleading information deliberately provided to the analyst (who does not realize someone is trying to deceive him or her).

These all-too-common errors can occur in any setting in which risk is being assessed. They are not confined to the national security arena.

The good news is that a number of techniques have been developed to help analysts overcome their cognitive biases. These techniques can be applied in a variety of risk management settings. One of the best-known techniques in intelligence analysis is the structured analysis of competing hypotheses (SACH), first developed in the 1970s by retired Central Intelligence Agency veteran Richards (Dick) J. Heuer, Jr. The first step in SACH is to identify all potential hypotheses, rather than starting with a likely or preferred hypothesis. Then the analyst lists evidence and arguments for and against each hypothesis. The next step, diagnostics, involves trying to disprove as many theories as possible by creating an evidence matrix using gathered information. The findings are reviewed, and identified gaps are filled during the refinement stage. Inconsistencies are then examined, with the view that less consistency results in less likelihood of a particular hypothesis being correct. At this point, the analyst uses his or her judgment to eliminate hypotheses. A sensitivity analysis is then conducted to weigh how conclusions would be affected by inaccurate key assumptions or evidence. Finally, those responsible for the analysis present conclusions to the decisionmaker, along with a summary of alternatives that were considered and rejected. By considering multiple hypotheses and applying the evidence across all of them, many cognitive errors can be avoided.

Obtaining Accurate Intelligence

The environment in which intelligence analysis is being conducted should be conducive to obtaining accurate results. Heuer recommends that a good management system do the following:

- "Encourage products that clearly delineate their assumptions and chains of inference and that specify the degree and source of uncertainty involved in the conclusions.

- Support analyses that periodically re-examine key problems from the ground up in order to avoid the pitfalls of the incremental approach.

- Emphasize procedures that expose and elaborate alternative points of view.

- Educate consumers about the limitations as well as the capabilities of intelligence analysis; define a set of realistic expectations as a standard against which to judge analytical performance."[3]

Although Heuer is specifically addressing intelligence analysis, these recommendations are important to consider when setting up a risk management structure and process.

It may be helpful to take a brief look at some domestic agencies that have been successfully using intelligence analysis to manage risk for some time. For example, the U.S. Coast Guard, in the conduct of its multi-mission maritime function, uses intelligence analysis in support of its living marine resources activities, including the establishment of specialized fishing zones and fish species analysis. The Coast Guard also uses intelligence analysis to support its environmental response to pollution by vessels, in particular the "fingerprinting" of oil residues left by vessels and pollution tracking in waterways. Other agencies, such as the Nuclear Regulatory Commission, the Department of Energy, the Treasury Department, and GAO have been known to use intelligence analysis, and it would be worthwhile to conduct case studies of these agencies to gather additional information on these uses.

Conclusion

In this time of intense scrutiny of the government's involvement in the private sector, citizens are looking for information on what return on investment they will see as a result of the infusion of federal funds into various industry sectors. The Obama administration has promised transparency. Private-sector trends in risk management point to similar scrutiny by boards of directors, stockholders, and regulatory agencies that want to see appropriate returns and strong management of risk. For managers in the public sector, greater adoption of accurate, easily consumable information on risk would increase understanding of both risks and how future risks can be mitigated.

Getting the right information at the right time will help you determine what safeguards you need to put in place to prevent situations in which your organization is unable to complete its critical functions successfully. Creating uniform yet flexible risk management structures throughout your organization and using established risk management and intelligence analysis techniques will enable you to address and adapt to a changing environment. The risk of not managing risk is simply too high to ignore.

Discussion Questions

1. What are the key tasks in each of the three phases of risk management: identification, measurement, and management?

2. What are some of the common attributes of effective risk management methods?

3. What are some of the common errors analysts make that lead to poor analysis and faulty conclusions?

4. How does the technique of SACH help overcome such analytic biases?

5. How can its management system increase an organization's likelihood of obtaining accurate results?

Notes

1. National Infrastructure Advisory Council, *Risk Management Approaches to Protection: Final Report and Recommendations by the Council* (Washington, D.C., October 11, 2005).
2. The Economist Intelligence Unit, "Best Practice in Risk Management: A Function Comes of Age," *The Economist* (May 2007). http://www.acelimited. com/NR/rdonlyres/7545D871-396C-43BF-B796-6C3BE7D4870C/0/RISK_ MANAGEMENT_290307may07.pdf (accessed September 18, 2009).
3. Center for the Study of Intelligence, Central Intelligence Agency, "Perception: Why Can't We See What Is There To Be Seen?" *Psychology of Intelligence Analysis* (1999). http://www.au.af.mil/au/awc/awcgate/ psych-intel/art5.html (accessed November 24, 2009).

Minimizing Risk to Recovery: Avoiding Fraud, Waste, and Abuse in Federal Recovery Project Spending

Robert Shea and Philip Kangas

Remember Hurricane Katrina? Devastated communities needed federal assistance immediately. The U.S. Congress and the Bush administration pushed federal disaster agencies to quickly spend a lot of money and get recovery activity on the ground. Taxpayers, however, needed to know that the government was spending public dollars effectively and with minimal waste, fraud, and abuse. At the time, the U.S. Office of Management and Budget (OMB) did what it could to balance these competing goals, but with scant success.[1] Unfortunately, massive waste occurred. [2]

The current economic crisis is similar in some ways to the Hurricane Katrina situation, but it is far larger in scale. The recently passed American Recovery and Reinvestment Act (known as the Recovery Act) is the largest U.S. government response to a national emergency, with funding levels that dwarf anything in our country's history. This time, OMB has issued explicit guidance on managing the spending of Recovery Act funds and has built specific controls into the process to maximize results.

With obligations of almost $800 billion, federal agencies are responsible for an incredible amount of new spending, some on old programs, some on new ones. In any case, such an increase in funding presents major challenges. Congress and the American people want Recovery Act dollars spent on projects that will create jobs in the near term, and agencies must ensure the distribution process is transparent and fair.

Pressure from the administration to spend Recovery Act dollars quickly will inevitably create risk. The U.S. Government Accountability Office (GAO) noted in a recent report to Congress that "the risk of fraud, waste, and abuse grows when billions of dollars are going out quickly, eligibility requirements are being established or changed, new programs are being created, or a mix of these characteristics [exist]."[3] External scrutiny will be intense, with oversight responsibilities spread across the Recovery Accountability and Transparency Board, GAO, agency-level inspectors general, the White House, and ultimately, citizens, through www.recovery.gov (see Figure 5-1).

Figure 5-1: Layers of Recovery Act Oversight

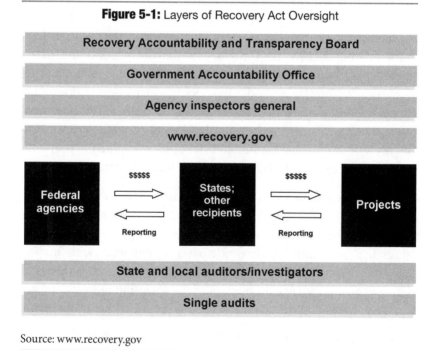

Source: www.recovery.gov

Recovery Act Goals

The Recovery Act lays out five clear goals:

- To preserve and create jobs and promote economic recovery

- To assist those most affected by the recession

- To make investments needed to increase economic efficiency by spurring technological advances in science and health

- To invest in transportation, environmental protection, and other infrastructure that will provide long-term economic benefits

- To stabilize state and local government budgets, in order to minimize or avoid reductions in essential services and counterproductive state and local tax increases.[4]

Taking a lesson from Katrina, OMB has provided detailed guidance on the reporting required of agencies and programs responsible for the success of Recovery Act spending. OMB, to enhance the chances of Recovery Act success, defines five accountability goals for its efforts:

- Funds are awarded and distributed in a prompt, fair, and reasonable manner.

- The recipients and uses of all funds are transparent to the public, and the public benefits of these funds are reported clearly, accurately, and in a timely manner.

- Funds are used for authorized purposes and potential for fraud, waste, error, and abuse is mitigated.

- Projects funded under this act avoid unnecessary delays and cost overruns.

- Program goals are achieved, including specific program outcomes and improved results on broader economic indicators.[5]

Measuring Risk and Performance

Performance benchmarks abound for agencies to gauge their success. OMB's guidance enumerates requirements for agencies to show that they are spending Recovery Act dollars wisely and with good results. So how should agencies, already stretched thin by copious audit, investigation, and reporting requirements, go about tackling these new and ambitious responsibilities?

OMB invites agencies to assess the risks to successful Recovery Act implementation and apply appropriate controls to mitigate those risks. In its April 2009 guidance, OMB asks agencies to assess those areas in which successful Recovery Act implementation is at greatest risk; apply appropriate controls to mitigate those risks; and periodically monitor and report progress. OMB developed a risk management framework (see Figure 5-2) to help agencies develop risk mitigation strategies and decide at what stages to employ and monitor specific controls.

Figure 5-2: OMB Risk Management Framework

	Preaward	Performance period		Past performance period
Strategic	Program outcomes and economic outcomes achieved			
	Competitive (and fixed-price) opportunities maxed			
	Wasteful spending, fraud, and abuse identified and minimized			
Operations	Funds obligated timely	Funds expended timely	Undelivered orders minimized	Sunset recovery requirements
	Improper payments minimized			
	Timely and accurate data reported to www.recovery.gov			
Reporting compliance	Agency and program plans approved	Agency and program plan milestones completed by estimated dates		
	Spend-plan approved	Spend-plan milestones completed by estimated dates		

Source: U.S. Office of Management & Budget, ARRA Guidance, April 2009

The framework divides risk mitigation strategies into three major implementation areas:

- **Strategic:** Meeting high-level goals

- **Operations:** Effectively and efficiently using resources

- **Reporting compliance:** Meeting applicable reporting requirements.

The framework further defines the periods of performance during which specific controls should be employed. For example, programs should ensure controls are in place to minimize fraud throughout the performance period, but should monitor obligation rates only until the performance period of a particular project begins.

Managing Internal Controls

OMB's provision for risk assessment is not a new requirement. Federal internal controls guidance has long emphasized understanding and addressing risk. GAO recently highlighted the need for internal controls to ensure that federal, state, and local governments use Recovery Act funds appropriately.[6] GAO had previously published standards for internal controls that addressed five key areas: the control environment, risk assessment, control activities, information and communication, and monitoring.[7]

- The **control environment** establishes clear accountability goals and reporting authorities to achieve established program outcomes.

- **Risk assessments** within internal controls include determining the probability of risks and their potential impact on a program.

- **Control activities** are essentially mitigation actions to prevent or address known risks.

- **Information and communication** enable responsible officials to make informed decisions on how best to apply resources to carry out their responsibilities.

- Program officials should structure **monitoring** activities to create a systematic review process whereby responsible officials not only receive but act on ongoing performance data.

OMB's direction is consistent with these guidelines.

Conducting a Gap Analysis

So where does an overwhelmed agency or program begin? First, it should conduct a gap analysis by taking the Recovery Act requirements and comparing them with the existing program capabilities. For example, the Recovery Act requires each agency to report job creation numbers directly linked to Recovery Act investments. If a program has never had to report this data, then a gap exists.

Note that a gap analysis need not be cumbersome or time-consuming. A simple inventory of Recovery Act and OMB guidance requirements—which can be done by surveying program managers—will help determine whether an agency is able to respond to either or both sets of requirements. Second, the gaps should be arrayed by factor to illustrate which areas pose the greatest risk to successful Recovery Act implementation. Factors may include the size or the age of the program, its significance with regard to the administration's recovery priorities, or whether an audit has found that problems are affecting the program's performance. OMB's guidance provides examples of some of the factors agencies might use to assess risk.[8]

Figure 5-3 illustrates one approach for performing a risk analysis to establish a clear risk mitigation approach. Based on this analysis, agencies and programs can better decide where to focus the most attention to mitigate risks. GAO suggests that control activities appropriate for Recovery Act funds include establishing policies, procedures, and guidelines that enforce management's directives and achieve effective internal controls over specific program activities. GAO provides examples of such policies and procedures that are particularly relevant to Recovery Act spending, including proper execution and accurate and timely recording of transactions and events, controls to help ensure compliance with program requirements, establishment and review of performance measures and indicators, and appropriate documentation of transactions and internal controls.[9]

Figure 5-3: Approach to Establishing Risk Mitigation Action Plan Based on Gap Analysis Findings

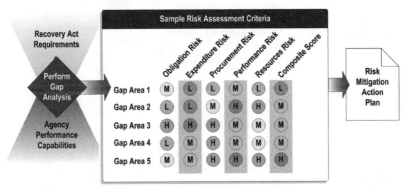

Source: U.S. General Accountability Office, Recovery Act, May 2009

Identifying Common Risks

It is simply not possible to give equal attention to all program areas and eliminate all threats to successful Recovery Act implementation. Doing so would bring activities to a halt—exactly the opposite of what is intended with the Recovery Act. That is why OMB invites agencies to take a reasonable approach to ascertaining where the greatest risks lie and applying mitigation strategies accordingly. This exercise is not just for the sake of compliance (though the documentation created is important evidence to show auditors and investigators when they come knocking); it is critical to the success of an agency's Recovery Act program.

Figure 5-4 identifies common risks associated with programs receiving stimulus funding, the impact of those risks, and best practice approaches for risk mitigation.

Figure 5-4: Best Practices for Mitigation of Common Risks Associated with Programs Receiving Stimulus Funding

Risk area	Impact of risk if not addressed	Mitigation strategy best practices
Programs receiving large stimulus allocations	• Insufficient resources and skills to handle workload • Application of funding to complex program needs may create tracking and reporting challenges that hinder clear understanding of performance results.	• Conduct skill gap analysis; adopt strategy to address all needed Recovery Act skills • Clarify a few critical performance metrics and tie spending to accountable program execution.
Program outputs/ outcomes not clearly defined	Projects will not achieve intended result.	Develop clear measures of program/project success in consultation with stakeholders.
Insufficient resources	Projects will not be completed adequately, or fewer projects will be completed adequately.	Seek specific training on accountability controls; engage OMB representatives frequently throughout process.
Financial management execution risk	Funds will be wasted; creates risk of improper payments.	Improve financial monitoring and control for payment accountability.
New programs lacking appropriate administrative structure	Insufficient administrative infrastructure may create incomplete or inaccurate reporting.	Create standardized templates for performance reporting; share lessons learned/best practices with agencies to enhance compliance.
Programs with history of cost/schedule overruns	Projects will be over budget and off schedule; funding of poor performing programs does not necessarily fix broken processes.	Adopt earned value management metrics for projects; target specific controls to address systemic issues impacting program performance.
Programs with ongoing/ outstanding audit findings	Program success will be impeded by management challenges.	Adopt fixes to audit findings; build audit response compliance actions into ongoing monitoring.

Risk area	Impact of risk if not addressed	Mitigation strategy best practices
Performance issues with funding recipients	Projects will not achieve intended results.	Establish performance-based expectations and tie to funding streams; provide additional resources/tools/ monitoring to funding recipients.
Lack of leading indicators of performance	Agency will realize problems after it is too late to fix them.	Adopt triggers to ascertain when projects are off track; clearly identify responsible parties to enhance accountability.

Keep in mind that if a program is small, with little expectation of job creation or retention, an agency or program may not need to devote significant resources to getting the most accurate estimates from the program. On the other hand, if it is a large, nationwide construction program with broad impact, then determining the probability of risk for key programmatic and financial elements and ensuring job creation is critical. In this case, the agency should invest whatever it takes to get the measurement right.

Final Thoughts

A comprehensive risk management plan should correctly prioritize program risks based on the probability and impact of each risk. Risk mitigation plans should likewise identify specific actions to reduce risk, the responsible parties for risk mitigation, a timeline for action planning, and specific expectations for risk-avoidance compliance reporting. GAO and other oversight bodies are actively working to identify and communicate such issues to OMB.[10] In the meantime, agencies should be prepared to propose a reasonable, achievable approach to documenting the effects of the stimulus.

Agencies are reeling from Recovery Act requirements. Responsible executives should leverage existing activities to minimize the burden. Most agencies already have a senior management council or equivalent whose job it is to ensure controls are in place and programs are working as intended. Agencies should employ such oversight mechanisms to drive compliance and address Recovery Act risks. Likewise, responsible program managers can use existing performance measures and reporting systems to report much or most of the data required by the Recovery Act, and financial and performance management professionals should track stimulus spending within existing systems. Agencies are not required to create duplicative systems or procedures for activities underway just to meet the requirements of the Recovery Act.

The ultimate goal of this endeavor is to accelerate the nation's economic recovery. OMB's guidance is a thoughtful and serious effort to mitigate known risks to the successful implementation of the act. While the requirements may seem overly prescriptive, agency executives can minimize the burden they pose if they approach the requirements in a methodical but reasonable way. That is all Congress, OMB, and other oversight entities require. During the Katrina response, surge funding lacked appropriate controls, fostering fraud, waste, and abuse. As we comply with the new Recovery Act requirements, we should all "remember Katrina."

Discussion Questions

1. What mistakes made in managing federal assistance in response to Hurricane Katrina can be avoided with Recovery Act spending?

2. What are the five accountability goals OMB has defined for Recovery Act spending? Are these relevant measures for success?

3. Will OMB's risk management framework prove useful in helping agencies decide when to employ and monitor specific controls? How?

4. When is a gap analysis called for, and how can it help mitigate risk?

5. What best risk management practices are recommended for programs with a history of cost/schedule overruns or ongoing/outstanding audit findings?

Notes

1. U.S. Office of Management and Budget, "Eligibility Verification Requirements for Delivery of Benefits to Victims of Hurricanes Katrina and Rita," (Washington, D.C., October 13, 2005), http://www.whitehouse. gov/omb/financial/fia/hurricanes_katrina_rita_10-13-05.pdf (accessed September 18, 2009).

2. United States Senate, Committee on Homeland Security and Governmental Affairs, "Hurricane Katrina: A Nation Still Unprepared," S. Rept. 109-322 (Washington, D.C., 2006), http://frwebgate.access.gpo.gov/cgi-bin/getdoc. cgi?dbname=109_cong_reports&docid=f:sr322.pdf (accessed September 18, 2009).

3. U.S. Government Accountability Office, "Recovery Act: GAO's Efforts to Work with the Accountability Community to Help Ensure Effective and Efficient Oversight," GAO-09-672T, (report on testimony before the Subcommittee on Investigations and Oversight, Committee on Science and Technology, U.S. House of Representatives, May 5, 2009), http://www.gao. gov/new.items/d09672t.pdf?source=ra.4 (accessed November 24, 2009).

4. The American Recovery and Reinvestment Act of 2009, Public Law 111-5, 111th Cong., 1st sess. (January 6, 2009), http://frwebgate.access.gpo.gov/cgi-bin/getdoc.cgi?dbname=111_cong_bills&docid=f:h1enr.txt.pdf (accessed September 18, 2009).

5. Peter R. Orzag, U.S. Office of Management and Budget, "Updated Implementing Guidance for the American Recovery and Reinvestment Act of 2009," (memorandum for the Heads of Departments and Agencies, M-09-15, Washington, D.C., April 3, 2009).

6. U.S. Government Accountability Office, "Recovery Act: As Initial Implementation Unfolds in States and Localities, Continued Attention to Accountability Issues Is Essential," GAO-09-580 (Washington D.C., April 2009).

7. U.S. Government Accountability Office, "Standards for Internal Control in the Federal Government," GAO/AIMD-00-21.3.1 (Washington, D.C., November 1999).

8. See note 5.

9. See note 6.

10. See note 3.

CHAPTER 6 ━━━━━━━━━━━━━━━

Managing a Governmental Health Plan

Sheila Beckett

In 1975, the Texas Legislature adopted recommendations from an interim study commission that I staffed, creating a uniform group insurance program. This program offered the customary benefits provided by an employer, the largest and most expensive being health insurance. Up until then, state agencies and institutions of higher education offered health insurance plans individually. These plans varied greatly based on the demographics of each agency's workforce and the level of appropriations made to each agency. As you can imagine, there was much inequity.

The statute passed by the legislature required that all executive, legislative, and judicial agencies participate in the new group insurance program. It allowed institutions of higher education to elect to participate in the new program or to continue offering separate health coverage. All of the state's institutions of higher education elected to participate, except the University of Texas system and the Texas A&M University system. Since the statute was passed, participation in the group insurance program has remained largely unchanged, except that certain county employees are now eligible.

The program is governed by the six-member Employees Retirement System (ERS) Board of Trustees. This board is made up of three active state employees elected from the system membership. The governor, the speaker of the state house of representatives, and the chief justice of the state supreme court each make an appointment to the board. The board appoints an executive director, who serves at the pleasure of the board.

The executive director is responsible for the day-to-day operations of the group benefits program (GBP).

The Group Benefits Program

As executive director of the Employees Retirement System of Texas from 1996 to 2004, I managed the state employees' and retirees' GBP, which provided health and dental coverage, life insurance, and short- and long-term disability insurance. The GBP provides health care coverage to over 500,000 Texas state employees, retirees, and family members. It is a pay-as-you-go system financed primarily by state appropriations, but also employee contributions for family member coverage and out-of-pocket payments for usage of health benefits. On average, this program spends over $2 billion annually, and the average annual increase in cost has been 10 percent.

In Texas, the GBP is statutorily designated as a trust. As such, the duty of care guiding principle is fiduciary duty. Common law defines a *fiduciary* as acting solely in the interest of beneficiaries, with the exclusive purpose of providing benefits that are earned or promised. Fiduciaries must carry out their duties in a prudent manner and transparently implement the program according to plan documents. Fiduciaries are charged with prudent management of program resources; therefore, they must be mindful of keeping administrative expenses at reasonable levels.

It's very important to develop consensus GBP policies to provide a guiding structure for decision-making. These policies must address the cost drivers of the GBP. Defining who may participate in the GBP is a fundamental policy that affects cost. A large, diverse pool of participants helps make health coverage more affordable. However, the policy-maker will want to maximize these outcomes by encouraging as close to 100 percent participation as possible and discouraging participants from making selections or choices that have negative financial consequences.

The policy must determine how risk is going to be managed and shared. Benefit coverage must be defined based on what is reasonable and affordable but should try to assure fairness to all participants when addressing the level and availability of health services. Finally, decision-makers should determine the total cost per individual that the system can afford. This could be done as a maximum average cost per person or as a percentage of the GBP budget or state budget.

It is the responsibility of the ERS executive director to guide the policy process and to achieve consensus on the policies affecting the GBP. The ERS executive director should develop policy options and recommended actions, then present the policy options and proposed actions to the governing board for consideration. A variety of briefing sessions should be scheduled to inform stakeholders about policies and options for changes. Stakeholders include leadership offices and key legislators, representatives of state agencies and higher education institutions, employees, and employee organizations.

Four Guiding Policies

Over the more than 30-year life of the Texas GBP, the health policies have evolved and strengthened. There are four primary guiding policies.

1. **Obtain 100 percent participation by all employees, retirees, and families, with the employer accepting most of the financial risk.** This is supported by state appropriations that provide full contribution for full-time employees and retirees and 50 percent contribution for family members. Part-time employees' premiums are partially covered by the state.

2. **Share the cost of using the health care benefit with the user.** A system of copays was developed for health care services and prescription drugs. Along with this cost-sharing scheme, maximum annual out-of-pocket costs were established.

3. **Ensure access to quality health care providers.** This was accomplished by requiring that health plans develop a broad network of doctors and hospitals and seek to maintain the network.

4. **Maintain a contingency reserve fund not exceeding 10 percent of expenditures.** This policy was authorized by statute but was difficult to implement due to the state's resource constraints. Although not fully understood or appreciated by budget writers, the reserve fund provides flexibility to manage the financial peaks and valleys of the program and is required by law for private insurance companies. Governments inherently have limited resources to allocate, and state government programs cannot run budget deficits or shortfalls. Therefore, careful budget estimates are prepared to ensure that expenditures do not exceed revenues plus balances and reserves.

Understanding Cost Drivers

Managing the GBP requires that the executive director understand the dynamics of the program and is knowledgeable about the cost drivers. *Cost drivers* are identifiable factors causing changes in expenditure patterns. Two factors explain most of the cost impact on an insurance program: participant demographics and the health condition of the participants. For example, if your participant pool is predominantly made up of women of childbearing age or people over age 50, the cost will be higher due to these demographics. If your participant pool includes a disproportionate number of people with diabetes or heart conditions, again, your cost will be higher.

The executive director of the ERS must know the participant demographics: age, sex, geographic location, and related trends and growth rates, and must track information regarding the health condition of participants, the most common and costly medical services, and prescription drugs.

He or she must develop, prescribe the format of, and collect, monitor, and analyze financial data, which should enable cost forecasting. ERS summarizes cost trends in three categories: medical care providers, hospital care at inpatient and outpatient facilities, and prescription drugs. Much has been written about the rising cost of medical services and prescription drugs. Like demographics and health status, these play an important role in the cost of a program and need to be monitored. Improvements in medical technology and prescription drugs are introduced continuously and play a significant role in improving health outcomes but also affect the cost of an insurance program. Finally, rates of consumption of medical services and prescription drugs must also be tracked.

Keys to Success

The GBP is one of the most successful programs in Texas state government. It is the health plan that others attempt to emulate or other groups of public-sector employees would like to join. There are several reasons that ERS has been able to sustain this reputation: balance, global coverage, communication, a good contracting process, transparency, and management of the appeals process.

Balance

We managed the program with an emphasis on the customer; this was balanced with being fiscally responsible. It is a challenge to achieve such balance because maintaining fiscal health is frequently incompatible with being customer-oriented. Over time, policymakers had emphasized benefits in lieu of salary increases. Employees saw this as one of the primary perks of state employment. We also understood the value of the large and diverse pool of participants; it allowed us to leverage a large pool of quality providers and obtain discounts for services. The pool was diverse in age, gender, ethnicity, and health condition. Adverse selection was moderated because the state paid the entire contribution cost for employees and retirees and half of the cost of dependent coverage—the only exposure to adverse selection.

ERS had a core group of talented, dedicated staff who possessed institutional knowledge essential to managing this complex program. Very importantly, ERS had expert assistance from a consulting actuarial firm that had worked with the program since 1974. There simply is no substitute for the experience, care, and perspective these advisors provided to the GBP.

The GBP health plans included a point of service (POS), self-insured plan financed through state appropriations and contributions from members for family coverage. This plan had a private-sector partner to administer the network of medical providers and to process the claims. We separated the prescription drug program (PDP) from the health plan and hired a separate benefit manager to develop the retail pharmacy network and mail pharmacy and to pay the claims for members. During the time that I managed the program, there were also health maintenance organization (HMO) choices. For a time, the GBP had a self-insured HMO. However, it was discontinued because the cost of benefits exceeded the cost of the POS plan. The other HMO options were commercial insurance products and were included in the portfolio of health plans if the cost of inclusion was equal to or less than the cost of the self-insured plan. It was very difficult for most HMOs to compete against the relatively low cost of the self-insured plan.

Providing Global Coverage

Providing global coverage was challenging. While most of the participants live in Texas, some employees have working assignments in other states. Retirees and family members live all over the world, so benefits must be portable. Participants living in Texas are spread throughout the large state, and there are few options for medical services in the more rural areas. We took care to provide these services globally.

A team of staff and consulting actuaries worked with an advisory board made up of health plan participants, industry experts, and the governing board to review the vision and direction for the global coverage health plan. The plan of benefits and incremental costs were evaluated on an annual basis, and rates were set by the ERS board of trustees annually. Most years, the plan of benefits did not need much revision, but the HMO plans were competitively bid each year. Because of the requirement that HMOs cost less than the self-insured plan, there was significant volatility in the HMO choices, making this a very difficult communication problem.

Twice during the time I was managing the plan, significant revisions to the benefit plan were required to cut the cost of the plan and balance the budget. Unfortunately, the changes usually resulted in more costs shifted to the participants. However, significant cost savings were also realized by renegotiating or rebidding the PDP and by renegotiating provider contracts. The POS plan administrator contract was competitively bid every three to six years. These changes were thoroughly vetted with the advisory committee, governing board, legislative staff and members, and other government leadership. In addition, forums were held to brief the participants and agency benefit coordinators.

Communication

Communication is key to managing any large public program, but it is even more essential for a health plan, which impacts people in the most personal and direct manner. Careful planning went into frequent communication with the financial partners—government leadership staff and other legislative leaders and staff. It was very important to identify and focus on key members of the governor's, lieutenant governor's, and speaker's offices, as well as the state senate and house of representatives. We made an effort to educate these government leaders more extensively so that they could act as advocates for the plan. We held regular meetings, delivered reports on the fiscal status of the health plan, and developed standardized report formats to promote consistency in the material we shared. Over time, this significantly helped our education effort. We also made sure to keep the employee and retiree association and groups informed. Keeping these groups as allies was paramount.

A Good Contracting Process

Develop a good contracting process for retaining your private-sector partners. This can be done by developing good contracts with performance standards and consequences and monitoring them closely. On a monthly basis, ERS senior staff met with the self-insured POS administrator and the PDP vendor. Program staff met with their working counterparts at least monthly. Operationally, we had daily contact with all the vendors as we actively managed the complex plans.

Each year, have the contracts audited by an outside, independent firm. Hold the vendors accountable. Don't be afraid to rebid or renegotiate the contracts. The health care market is very dynamic, and going out for bids allows you to take advantage of improvements. Often, you can lower your costs without too much difficulty.

Transparency

Managing a government health plan is more complex than managing one in the private sector. There's more transparency in a government plan: All documents, except for private health information, are subject to disclosure. We regularly disclosed information to government and legislative leaders, employee and retiree groups, and the press. The pool of participants is more complex; it includes all elected officials, legislators, judges, and their family members. The participants tend to have a more sophisticated understanding of their benefits—especially employees and retirees of the higher education system. Because Texas has tended to use benefits as a significant form of compensation, often in lieu of salary increases, employees and retirees pay close attention to any changes that they think dilute the benefit.

Policy decisions affecting a government health plan, including benefit changes, selection of health and prescription drug plan vendors, and rates paid for each category of coverage, require governing board approval. Board members are trained to understand the laws and budget of the health plan. These briefings cover the components of the health plan's cost and the benefit structure. Board members meet at an annual workshop to receive in-depth information in an informal setting. This allows free and wide-ranging discussion among board members, senior staff, and invited experts and advisors. Board members are given one-on-one briefings as appropriate or requested. Also, during the regularly scheduled formal meetings of the board, additional information about the health plan is conveyed, often through the deliberation of appeals by participants regarding denial of benefits.

Managing the Appeals Process

ERS has a formal appeals process for the denial of health benefits. If the appeal is upheld at any point in the process, the claim is paid. The first appeal is a request that the health plan reconsider its decision. If that is unsuccessful, the participant may file an appeal to ERS. Staff will consider the denial and make a decision. If approved, the claim will be paid. If not, the staff will refer the appeal to the ERS Medical Board. The medical board may recommend that the claim be paid or denied. If the staff and medical board recommend denial, the executive director may override the decision and pay the claim.

If the executive director agrees with the recommendation to deny, a letter is sent to the participant informing him or her that the denial stands but that he or she has the right to an administrative appeal conducted by the state office of administrative hearings. Then, at a formal hearing of the board, the examiner presents the case, allowing for testimony by the participant and ERS staff and/or health plan vendor representatives. The board makes a final decision about whether benefits will be awarded, which can be appealed to the state district court. The court system process makes the final decision in these cases. Fortunately, very few cases have administrative appeals, and even fewer are appealed through the court system.

Reflection

Successfully managing the Texas GBP was the most challenging and rewarding experience in my career. The importance of this program in the everyday lives of state employees, retirees, and their families was a constant reminder of my fiduciary duty. And with the current national debate over health care reform, the GDP case illustration underscores the importance of good policy models.

I have two disappointments looking back over my years of managing the Texas GDP. First, we were unsuccessful in gaining support from budget writers for a healthcare spending target. And second, we were not able to convince budget writers of the necessity to fully comply with the statutory requirement of a contingency reserve fund. Without these tools to assist us in managing the program, our flexibility and efficiency was reduced.

Discussion Questions

1. Identify and discuss some of the major features of the Texas statewide Group Health Benefit Insurance Program.

2. What is the composition of the ERS Board of Trustees? What are the major responsibilities of the Director of ERS?

3. Define and discuss the fiduciary concept. What are some major fiduciary responsibilities?

4. What are the four guiding policies under which the ERS operates? Why are these policies so important to the creation of a successful system? Why is the Texas GBP so successful?

5. Identify and discuss the importance and value of a good contracting process. Why is transparency such an important factor?

PART 3

Strategic Human Capital Management

CHAPTER 7 ⎯⎯⎯⎯⎯⎯⎯⎯⎯⎯⎯⎯⎯

A Road Map for Federal Strategic Human Capital Planning

William Trahant

Increasingly, federal agencies are developing strategic human capital (HC) plans to help them meet changing mission requirements and take a purposeful, long-term approach to HC management. The drive to do so is determined by several factors:

- The need for agencies to accurately forecast their future HC requirements based on the anticipated departure of thousands of baby boomers from government in the years ahead

- The need to streamline hiring and make government an "employer of choice" that is able to accommodate surges in job applications in economic downturns, as well as hire the best workers and compete with the private sector when the economy is strong

- The need for federal HC professionals to manage HC issues in a more comprehensive way, starting with recruitment and hiring, and encompassing retention, training, performance management, leadership development, succession planning, and employee retirement

- The HC requirements of the Obama administration, the Chief Human Capital Officers (CHCO) Act of 2002, and the Human Capital Assessment and Accountability Framework (HCAAF), the road map created by the U.S. Office of Personnel Management (OPM) for transforming HC management in government.

Successful Strategic HC Planning

What exactly *is* strategic human capital planning (SHCP), and what are the critical factors in effectively implementing SHCP within a federal agency? SHCP is a comprehensive, structured approach to assessing an organization's current and long-term HC needs and making plans to meet them. It begins with thorough analysis of current workforce data—including demographic profiling, skill gap analysis, work climate assessment, and performance management analysis—and identifies the gaps between current capabilities and future needs. It then makes clear commitments to specific goals and objectives that close identified skill gaps and completes the process by developing implementation plans and assigning accountability for specific results.

To be successful, strategic human capital planning must:

- Focus on implementation

- Be tightly targeted in scope

- Be future oriented

- Make senior leaders accountable for results

- Create a clear set of planning steps.

Focus on Implementation

Most planning initiatives focus lots of time on plan formulation but don't put enough emphasis on translating the good intentions of the formulated plan into action and results. Consequently, as agency leaders think about implementing strategic HC plans, it's essential they follow through on commitments and set up the infrastructure to effect full implementation.

Tightly Target the Scope

Frequently, strategic planning activities generate numerous commitments (a.k.a. goals and objectives). But generating too many goals can be self-defeating because it dilutes the ability of an agency to focus on just a few strategic priorities. One way an agency's leaders can limit the focus of HC planning efforts is to be certain all commitments are directly mission driven. If leaders can't directly link a goal to the agency's mission, they shouldn't include it as a planning objective.

Be Future Oriented

Some planning efforts deal with solving today's problems in the future. In contrast, strategic human capital planning focuses on solving *tomorrow's* issues today. Thus, an agency's leaders must carefully answer certain key questions to ensure that planning efforts are truly future oriented. Among the questions to ask: "What will happen in five years if we continue to manage our HC resources the same way we manage them today?" And "What does our workforce *need* to look like in five years in terms of competencies, tenure, age, and diversity for us to fulfill our agency's public mission?" As part of answering such questions, planners should review their agency's strategic business plan and prepare responses in the context of that document.

Make Leaders Accountable for Results

HC planning is typically seen as the province of the human resources (HR) department. HR professionals do have an important role to play in supporting the HC planning process: providing HR data, designing defensible studies, and (in the federal government) advising on OPM and HCAAF requirements.

But HC management is a staff function that can't drive organizational change by itself. By contrast, an organization's line leaders have formal authority to effect real change in organizations. Not only do they possess daily decision-making power, they also have direct accountability for the actions they take. Consequently, it's important that an agency's line leaders be held accountable for HC plan implementation because they have the position power to influence others, align and assign resources, and follow through on HC issues. Accountability is further heightened when goals and objectives focus on specific, measurable, and time-bounded results.

Create a Clear Set of Planning Steps

A good planning process begins with the end in mind—a clear statement of the desired outcome (result) and a clear description of the steps required to get there. Good planning also follows a distinct road map. When that road map is graphically depicted, it helps focus people's attention on key activities and milestones.

With that in mind, look at Figure 7-1. Here you see various *inputs to planning* that are key to shaping the planning process at the start of a planning initiative. Next, agency leaders must articulate specific HC goals, metrics, strategies for achieving goals, and implementation plans. These represent specific *commitments to action*. Finally, leaders must put certain *implementation enablers* in place to move from successful planning to effective plan implementation.

Figure 7-1: Federal Sector Strategic Human Capital Planning Model

Inputs to Planning

In the inputs to planning phase, an agency's leaders undertake eight critical activities:

1. **Conducting a workforce analysis.** This involves a comprehensive assessment of an organization's workforce, including consideration of factors like workforce age and gender diversity and work-related elements like tenure and turnover. An analysis of these factors can yield a profile of an agency's current and anticipated future HC resources.

2. **Reviewing relevant business plans.** Successful HC plans align human resources in pursuit of strategic business goals. Accordingly, a careful review of an agency's strategic business plan can identify the business challenges and commitments for which human capital is required and organized within an agency. It can then shape the definition of HC initiatives to address these challenges and recommend how resources should be allocated to address critical HC requirements.

3. **Factoring HCAAF requirements into SHCP.** OPM has published a comprehensive framework for monitoring progress in HC management: the Human Capital Assessment and Accountability Framework. The five major HCAAF elements provide an organizing framework for identifying commitments in an agency's strategic HC plan.

4. **Reviewing third-party analyses.** Public scrutiny of federal agencies yields independent assessments that affect HC management. For example, studies by the U.S. Government Accountability Office (GAO) and score reports from OMB-PART (the U.S. Office of Management and Budget Program Assessment Rating Tool), which assess agency program effectiveness, offer important insights into the challenges that should be addressed in an agency's strategic HC plan.

5. **Undertaking an HC future scan.** This exercise asks agency decisionmakers to anticipate future trends and factors that will affect their agency before they define strategic goals and objectives.

6. **Completing an HC strengths, weaknesses, opportunities, and threats (SWOT) analysis.** This involves synthesizing all current-state assessments into one set of conclusions, as well as looking internally to determine what strengths and weaknesses affect the agency's management of its human capital. It also involves looking externally to determine what opportunities and threats to effective HC management exist in the agency's environment.

7. **Incorporating commercial best practices.** Private-sector organizations often experiment with innovative HC practices, and government agencies can benefit from examining the most successful of these. Many won't meet government requirements or operating constraints, but some may unfreeze thinking and offer new ways of operating.

8. **Assessing current HR programs.** A popular way to initiate the strategic HC planning process is to conduct a baseline assessment of HR functions to assess the ways in which HR currently meets the needs of customers in an agency's various business units.

Commitments to Action

Next comes the commitments to action phase. This phase includes:

- **Vision setting.** It's critical that agency leaders articulate a vivid, specific description of the desired outcome the agency is seeking to accomplish with SHCP.

- **Setting strategic goals.** Establishing HC goals is the primary way to achieve an agency's HC vision. It requires discipline and organizational focus to create goals that are directly linked to the HC vision and, in turn, to the agency's mission. A good way to guide the definition of HC goals is to look at HCAAF requirements and ask: "How can our agency address HCAAF requirements in a succinct way?"

- **Defining plan metrics.** For each HC goal, agency executives should develop metrics by which work toward accomplishing that goal will be evaluated. Metrics focus an agency's leaders on specific measurable results they want to achieve.

■ **Creating strategies to achieve goals.** A strategy statement outlines the basic approach an agency will take to reach a goal.

■ **Defining objectives.** Objectives are the specific means by which each HC goal is accomplished. They represent one more level of granularity in the planning process beyond the setting of strategies. Objectives operationalize outlined strategies into statements that delineate who will do what by when.

Implementation Enablers

All agencies experience some difficulty in following through on strategic plan commitments, so it's important to include other elements in the SHCP process to facilitate plan implementation. These include:

■ **Accountability plans.** The HCAAF prescribes development of an accountability plan for all HC initiatives. Accountability plans detail the planning process. Typically, they take major initiatives and break them down into specific, short-term actions and results. They stipulate who is accountable for specific results and the timeframe for completion.

■ **Assignment of HC plan champions.** HC strategic plans often suffer from lack of effective follow-through, so it's important to assign plan champions responsible for full implementation in specific areas. *Champions* are senior executives, assigned by the senior HC decision-making team and accountable to it, who are responsible for clearing away obstacles to plan implementation and providing resources for plan completion. They are people who regularly report to the senior decision-making team and who have sufficient authority, organizational experience, and accountability to drive achievement of specific plan outcomes.

- **Progress reporting.** To support the work of HC plan champions, it's important to put a formal process in place to monitor progress on a regular basis. Are champions making progress in achieving their assigned goals? What obstacles, if any, are they encountering as they work to achieve specific HC outcomes? Progress reporting helps busy administrators keep a focus on plan implementation—to identify areas of success as well as issues that may be impeding successful rollout of HC initiatives.

- **Change management.** Strategic HC planning is a broad-based organizational initiative that often involves transformation of an agency's culture. To achieve this requires the cooperation of all organization employees. To secure that cooperation, senior leaders must be highly involved as SHCP champions, communicating the importance of SHCP to all employees and making the case for why it is important to the accomplishment of the agency's public mission.

- **Communication strategy.** It's also important to put communication strategies in place to drive changes in people's attitudes and work behaviors and to create employee buy-in for new HC practices. Organizational research shows that strategic messaging to employees during times of change enhances employee engagement with business priorities and helps create tight employee alignment with organizational goals.

- **Project management.** Finally, successful implementation of strategic HC plans must be undergirded by a strong project management mindset, one that links individual HC goals and initiatives to overarching organizational priorities. A strong project management approach also increases the likelihood of sustained success with SHCP by codifying the use of specific HC best practices, facilitating continuous improvement in the administration of all HR processes, and aligning employees with the organizational mission.

Conclusion

Effective strategic HC planning consists of structured decision-making around specific HC goals and calls for strong leadership accountability and plan monitoring to increase the probability of successful plan implementation.

SHCP will assume increasing importance in the federal government in the years ahead, as government executives grapple with the HC ramifications of the looming "retirement cliff"; as government agencies increasingly compete with the private sector to hire new generations of college graduates; as the federal government deals with expanding agency missions in areas such as defense, intelligence, and homeland security; and as the White House, Congress, and American taxpayers continue to demand that government agencies focus on performance, accountability, transparency, and results.

Discussion Questions

1. What is strategic human capital planning and what are the critical factors in effectively implementing it within a federal agency?

2. What are the drivers of federal strategic human capital planning?

3. What are the critical steps in implementing strategic human capital planning?

4. What eight input tasks are critical to successful human capital planning?

5. What enablers are critical to successful implementation?

CHAPTER 8

Fostering Professional Development through Certified Public Manager Programs

Howard R. Balanoff

The American Society for Public Administration (ASPA) advocates greater efficiency and effectiveness in all levels of government and encourages the spread of good public administration practices through its local chapters and national sections. A strong code of ethics and a variety of publications also promote the spread of best practices in public service. Through its collaboration with the National Certified Public Manager (CPM) Consortium and the ASPA Section on Certified Public Management (which now has more than 500 members across the country), the organization is in a position to promote even greater professional development in the field. The best example of ASPA and CPM collaboration is occurring in Texas, which is quickly becoming the cooperative model for such programs across the United States.

The CPM Program

The CPM program has been operating in the United States for about 30 years. It began in Georgia in 1979 as a certification program for public managers in state government. Initially, it spread throughout the southern states (i.e., Louisiana, Mississippi, and Arkansas) and eventually to all regions in the United States. By 1995, the CPM program had expanded to other states, including New Jersey, Texas, Arizona, and Washington, D.C., and local, federal, and nonprofit employees were participating. By

1996, the Graduate School of the U.S. Department of Agriculture (USDA) was delivering a CPM program to federal employees, and the Texas CPM program was training significant numbers of local government employees in addition to serving state, federal, and nonprofit employees. By 2009, about 40 CPM programs were in operation. CPM had also spread to California and New York.

The CPM program's primary goal is to improve the performance of public-sector managers and the organizational performance of state, local, and federal government employees. It is a comprehensive course of study by which public managers can acquire and apply best practices and theory to their management behaviors and strategies, all the while using prescribed sets of professional standards often called *competencies*. Those who complete the program earn the national trademarked designation of Certified Public Manager.

National Certified Public Manager Consortium

CPM programs in the United States operate under the umbrella of the National Certified Public Manager® Consortium, which establishes and preserves standards for the CPM designation. The consortium also monitors and accredits all CPM programs in the United States. Only accredited CPM programs are authorized to award the designation, which is trademarked to the consortium and its member programs. As is the case with other certification systems, accredited CPM programs are reviewed every five years for continued compliance with national CPM standards and reaccredited.

ASPA's Section on Certified Public Management

In early 2007, ASPA created the Section on Certified Public Management (SCPM; http://www.aspaonline.org/scpm). The Section is open to CPM alumni, students, and faculty and to all ASPA members who are interested in the concepts, principles, and practices of certified public management. The goal of this ASPA section is to promote the professional development and training of public and nonprofit managers in the ethical values and technical competencies associated with outstanding public service. The section also encourages cooperation and linkages with and between local ASPA chapters and CPM programs throughout the country. Another of its goals is to promote the growth and establishment of CPM programs in states that are not currently members of the National CPM Consortium.

Emphasis on Public-Sector Ethics and Integrity

One of the major contributions of the CPM program has been its emphasis on building strong ethical values into public-sector workplaces. For example, the CPM program in Texas has adopted the ethical values and competencies advocated by both the International City/County Management Association (ICMA) and the Texas City Management Association (TCMA). These competencies are designed to be applicable in a diverse, multi-sector workforce composed of people ranging from entry-level employees and contractors to senior executives reporting to elected and appointed officials.

Integrity

According to ICMA and TCMA, there are three distinct types of integrity:

- **Personal integrity.** Demonstrating accountability for personal actions; conducting personal relationships and activities fairly and honestly.

- **Professional integrity.** Conducting professional relationships and activities fairly, honestly, legally, and in conformance with the ICMA Code of Ethics (which requires knowledge of administrative ethics, specifically the ICMA Code of Ethics).

- **Organizational integrity.** Fostering ethical behavior throughout the organization through personal example, management practices, and training (requires knowledge of administrative ethics, ability to instill accountability in operations, and ability to communicate ethical standards and guidelines to others).

CPM programs focus on the importance of ethical behavior by introducing participants to the ethical codes of conduct of several organizations, such as ASPA, the ICMA, and the Government Finance Officers Association (GFOA). A variety of case studies also are taught in the classroom to illustrate the importance and complexity of ensuring ethical behavior in governmental organizations and among governmental contractors and subcontractors. Many case studies come from ASPA publications, such as the *Public Administration (PA) Times,* which features "The Ethics Corner." ASPA's journal, *Public Integrity,* also features articles and discussions involving ethical dilemmas and situations facing public managers.

In Texas, CPM programs are often conducted for a public-sector organization's entire management team, which reinforces the ethical culture for the entire local government community. The cities of Laredo, San Angelo, Abilene, and Waco have all sent employees to CPM training.

Technical Competencies

Let's look at some of the more important technical competencies public managers need to be successful. Again, the CPM program competencies mirror and build on competencies that have been adopted and advocated by the ICMA and TCMA. Required competencies identified by CPM, ASPA, ICMA, and TCMA that are relevant for local, state, and federal employees include:

- **Staff effectiveness.** Promotes the development and performance of staff and employees throughout the organization. It requires a knowledge of interpersonal relations, skill in motivation techniques, and the ability to identify others' strengths and weaknesses. Practices that contribute to this competency are coaching and mentoring, team leadership, empowerment, and delegation.

- **Functional and operational expertise and planning.** Includes functional/operational expertise, including understanding the basic principles of service delivery in functional areas and operational planning. It also includes skill in identifying and understanding trends and predicting the consequences of management and budgetary decisions on customer satisfaction and program service delivery.

- **Technological literacy.** Demonstrates an understanding of information technology and ensuring that IT is incorporated appropriately into plans and programs to improve service delivery, information sharing, organizational communication, and citizen access.

- **Budgeting and financial analysis.** Involves preparing and administering the budget. It requires knowledge of budgeting principles and practices, revenue sources, projection techniques, and financial control systems. Also required is skill in communicating financial information. Financial analysis involves interpreting financial information to assess the short-term and long-term fiscal condition of the community, determine the cost-effectiveness of programs, and compare alternative strategies. It requires knowledge of analytic techniques and skill in applying them.

- **Advocacy and interpersonal communication.** Covers facilitating the flow of ideas and information and fostering understanding between and among individuals, which are critical public management skills emphasized by ASPA, ICMA, TCMA, and CPM program courses. Advocating effectively in the public interest requires knowledge of interpersonal and group communication principles, such as skill in listening, speaking, and writing and the ability to persuade without diminishing the views of others. Advocacy involves communicating personal support for policies, programs, or ideals that serve the best interests of the local, state, or national community. Interpersonal communication involves exchanging verbal and nonverbal messages with others in a way that demonstrates respect for the individual and furthers organizational and community objectives. It requires ability to receive verbal and nonverbal cues and requires skill in selecting the most effective communication method for each interchange.

Best Practices

CPM provides the professional development and education programs, but the program relies heavily on ASPA sections (especially ASPA's CPM Section), ASPA chapters (such as Centex, Corpus Christi, Rio Grande Valley) and good-governance publications like ASPA's *Public Administration Review (PAR), PA Times, Public Integrity,* and *The Public Manager,* among others, to implement its training mission in Texas. To effectively implement the ethical values and technical competencies identified above requires a successful partnership with and between organizations such as CPM, ASPA, and ICMA. If each of these organizations tried a "go it alone" approach, their efforts would not be adequate to the task.

Texas

One of the best examples of such a partnership is in Texas, where ASPA, the Texas CPM program, and TCMA have combined forces to create one of the most successful professional development and education programs in the country. The CPM program is considered the premier professional development and educational service provider for public managers in the state. CPM participants receive ASPA membership at no additional cost, have access to ASPA publications, and can participate in ASPA chapters and sections.

At the local level, cities in Texas that have contracted with the Texas CPM program to promote ethics in the workplace and improve the technical skills and competencies of their managers and supervisors include Austin, San Antonio, Laredo, Waco, McAllen, Lubbock, San Angelo, and Abilene. Texas state agencies that send their managers and employees to Texas CPM programs include the Texas Commission on Environmental Quality (TCEQ), the Employee Retirement System (ERS) of Texas, and the Texas State Comptroller's Office. Federal organizations with operations in Texas that have sent employees to CPM programs include the U.S. Postal Service (USPS) and military and civilian agencies in the greater San Antonio area.

All levels of government in Texas are pleased with the success of the CPM program. It continues to have the bipartisan support of both liberal and conservative politicians as well as Texas professional public managers at all levels. Every year, two CPM graduations are held in the Texas Capitol; over the 12-year life of the CPM program, more than 900 participants have graduated. Graduation speakers have included the governor of Texas, the lieutenant governor of Texas, U.S. congresspeople, and Texas state legislators.

Florida

CPM programs are providing outstanding professional development and educational services to public-sector employees in Florida, too. In Florida, the CPM program has been a major provider of professional development and education in the public sector for more 20 years, especially for employees of the state's criminal justice system.

District of Columbia

The District of Columbia is yet another example of a CPM success story. The city has run a CPM program for Washington, D.C., employees for more than ten years. The program began with a multimillion-dollar grant from the not-for-profit sector. The purpose of the grant was to provide the city with the funds to promote an ethical culture and implement the technical skills and values associated with outstanding service to the public.

More Information

Readers are invited to find out more about how innovative programs such as the CPM program, ASPA, and the ICMA are making a positive impact on the professional development and education of public employees by visiting the organizations' websites:

- National CPM site: www.cpmconsortium.org
- National ASPA site: www.aspanet.org
- ICMA site: www.icma.org.

For information about how CPM and ASPA are combining to make a major difference in the education and training of the public-service workforce, go to:

- The ASPA CPM Section website: http://www.aspaonline.org/scpm

- The Texas Certified Public Manager site: http://www.txstate.edu/cpm.

Discussion Questions

1. What are the key aspects of the CPM program?

2. What are the key mission and activities of ASPA?

3. Discuss some of the collaborative efforts that have taken place between ASPA and the CPM program. Which states have served as models for these collaborative efforts? What are some of their accomplishments?

4. Why are ethics and ethics training considered to be major elements for both CPM and ASPA?

5. Identify and discuss some of the technical competencies that are so important for public managers.

CHAPTER 9

Fostering Ethics and Accountability in the Public-Sector Workplace

Bart Bevers

On May 3, 1987, the *Miami Herald* published a story alleging an affair between presidential candidate Gary Hart and a 29-year-old model named Donna Rice. Shortly thereafter, the *National Enquirer* published a now infamous photograph of the two. Less than a week later, polls in New Hampshire showed that Hart's support had been cut in half, dropping from 32 to 17 percent. Suddenly, he was 10 points behind Massachusetts governor Michael Dukakis. On May 8, 1987, Hart dropped out of the race.

More than 10 years later, in January 1998, President Bill Clinton was accused of having an affair with Monica Lewinsky. In the three months that followed this breaking story, President Clinton enjoyed a 73 percent approval rating, the highest of his eight-year administration. What happened during this 10-year period is uncertain. We might argue that what used to be unacceptable was now acceptable. America had changed. More recently, the American public has been subjected to an increasing number of ethical scandals, including those involving governors Eliot Spitzer, Rod Blagojevich, and Mark Sanford; evangelist Ted Haggard; and investor Bernie Madoff. Within the past two years, the federal government has bailed out financial institutions such as Bear Stearns, Fannie Mae, Freddie Mac, and AIG and allowed others, such as Lehman Brothers, to fail.

What happened to "right" and "wrong"? Why was "wrong" now becoming "right"? Why do people wait until *after* their secret lives are revealed to the public to change their behavior? Why did the federal government follow one standard to bail out some organizations and another to allow similarly situated entities to fail? Where is the consistency?

Public Trust

Public trust is the glue that holds our democracy together, but right now it seems to be at an all-time low. The roots of public trust are established in the soil of *integrity* and *accountability*. It cannot grow and thrive in the current fallow ground. Public trust cannot be generated from feel-good statements because many of these statements lack moral validity.

Great American leaders have acknowledged the need for public trust for decades. Before James Madison became president of the United States, he said, "The circulation of confidence is more important than the circulation of money."[1] Other former presidents have made similar statements:

> *Lyndon Baines Johnson:* Where government is based on the consent of the governed, every citizen is entitled to have complete confidence in the integrity of his government. Each individual officer, employee, or adviser of government must help to earn and must honor that trust by his own integrity and conduct in all official actions (Executive Order 11222, Standards of Ethical Conduct for Government Officers and Employees).

> *James Garfield:* Now more than ever before, the people are responsible for the character of their Congress. If that body be ignorant, reckless, and corrupt, it is because the people tolerate ignorance, recklessness, and corruption. If it be intelligent, brave, and pure, it is because the people demand these high qualities to represent them in the national legislature.... If the next centennial does not find us a great nation, it will be because those who represent the enterprise, the culture, and the morality of the nation do not aid in controlling the political forums.[2]

Accountability and the Subcomponents of Morals: Ethics, Values, and Principles

Accountability is defined in *Webster's American Dictionary* as "the quality or state of being accountable; *especially* an obligation or willingness to accept responsibility or to account for one's actions." It is defined in *Answers Dictionary* as "[t]he state of being accountable; liability to be called on to render an account; the obligation to bear the consequences for failure to perform as expected."

The key components of accountability are (1) an obligation or willingness to accept responsibility, (2) an obligation or willingness to account for one's actions, and (3) answerability. *Webster's American Dictionary* aptly indicates, by omission of a synonym for the word, there are no substitutes for accountability.

Ethics has been defined as "a branch of philosophy that is the systematic study of reflective choice, of the standards of right and wrong by which it is to be guided, and of the goods toward which it may ultimately be directed."[3] *Principles* are "the means of analysis (ways of thinking about moral problems)."[4] *Values* are the "criteria for 'good and evil.'"[5]

Webster's defines *morals* as:

a. of or relating to principles of right and wrong in behavior: ethical <*moral* judgments>
b. expressing or teaching a conception of right behavior <a *moral* poem>
c. conforming to a standard of right behavior
d. sanctioned by or operative on one's conscience or ethical judgment <a *moral* obligation>
e. capable of right and wrong action <a *moral* agent>.

The broader definition of *morals* includes ethics ("ethical"), principles ("principles of right and wrong"), and values ("standard of right behavior") (see Figure 9-1.)

Subjective Standards vs. Objective Standards

Understanding the difference between subjective standards and objective standards is not difficult. You need only watch America's most popular television show, *American Idol*. At the beginning of every season, thousands of people who sincerely, subjectively believe they can sing and hope to become the new *American Idol* winner audition for the show. Most of the contestants are sincerely wrong about their level of talent, which they discover when they are confronted with the more objective scrutiny of Simon Cowell and his team of judges.

Figure 9-1: Components of Morals

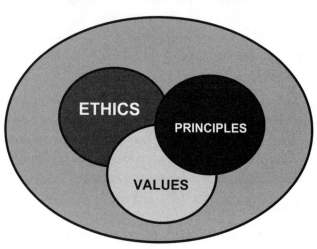

And anyone who has attempted to lose weight can tell you that true success is defined only by objective standards. One may not subjectively feel overweight. But a tape measure or a bathroom scale is an objective, and far better, indicator of whether one needs to lose weight.

Ethics in American government are no different. Subjective standards are illusory; they can be used to rationalize almost any behavior. Objective standards promote fair and equitable enforcement. Also, subjective standards are susceptible to change without notice, while objective standards are clear and can be measured. In moral and ethical decision-making, if the standard employed cannot be measured, that standard is subjective.

Strategically, the key to addressing ethical and moral issues in the public sector should be prevention, not merely after-the-fact enforcement. Effective prevention necessitates hiring and maintaining (1) ethical supervisors who model the appropriate behavior, (2) employees who understand the objective standards that management clearly communicates to them, and (3) supervisors who keep their eye on the ball, ensuring fair and equitable enforcement even in the face of compelling subjective rationalizations. But a good ethics policy is not enough.

Integrity

The Great Wall of China is one of the greatest construction feats in human history. It was built to keep the invading armies from the north at bay. It is 4,163 miles long, 15 to 30 feet thick at every point, and 25 feet tall. Centuries ago, it was guarded by more than one million soldiers at a time—or one soldier every 22 feet.

The wall is too long to go around, too high to go over, and too thick to drill through. So how did three invading armies get past it in the first 150 years of its existence, when it was guarded by more than one million soldiers? They bribed the guards at the gate. Picture the invading armies marching through the gates of a seemingly impenetrable wall—right in front of thousands of soldiers whose sole mission was to prevent those armies from doing exactly what they were doing.

Good policies are only as good as the integrity of those who enforce them—much like the Great Wall of China was only as strong as the integrity of the guards at the gates. Programs are good. Audit plans, work plans, investigative plans, strategic plans, resources, and people to carry out those plans are all good, but they are not the answer. These are what public administrators typically focus on when the conversation turns to integrity and accountability. They are all important bricks in the wall, but they are only as strong as the personal integrity of the people who use them and report the results.

Decision-Making on Ethical and Moral Issues

Non-moral decisions include the following:

- Should I wear brown socks or black socks today?
- Should I break up with my boyfriend (or girlfriend)?
- Should I go to a public or private university?

Moral issues involve absolutes, principles, values, and ethics and include questions like these:

- Should I take something that does not belong to me?
- Should I cheat on my income tax return?
- Can I lie about X and get by with it?
- Should I ignore this injustice?
- Should I cheat on my spouse or significant other?

Moral Decisions

Moral decisions are the decisions that shape the courses of our lives. They also affect the lives of others. Moral decisions are like the rudder on a large ship—seemingly small and unnoticeable, yet guiding the direction of the entire ship.

What we see, we think about. What we think about, we meditate on. What we meditate on, we eventually act on. Our actions form the foundation for our habits. Our habits shape our character, and our character determines our destiny. For example, if five years from now, I weigh 600 pounds, I would be responsible for that weight gain. There would be no one else to blame because I made the decisions that put me there. If I allow myself to look too frequently at the wrong foods, it will be only a matter of time before I think, meditate, and act upon those thoughts. Eating the wrong foods could turn into a habit—and could triple my weight. Remember, we are all responsible for our actions.

Character Formation

The formation of our character and our accompanying destinies is an iterative process. Briefly, the process is (1) look → (2) think → (3) meditate → (4) actions → (5) habits → (6) character → (7) destiny. True, lasting transformation requires an acknowledgement of this process. The genesis of true transformation occurs within, not externally. Real transformation begins with the renewing of your minds, but this truth alone will not set you free to change your destiny. You have to *know* this truth first. For example, I have a lock on the fence that leads to our backyard. A combination is required to open the lock. The mere truth that a combination for the lock exists will not let you into our backyard; you have to know the combination before you can be "set free" into our backyard. Truth never set anyone free until he or she took the time to know that truth.

The same holds true for the process of character formation. Creating true, lasting change necessitates that we look and think differently. We have to look at certain things we may not have looked at before and refuse to look at others. We have to decide to think about what is good and refuse to think about what we should not ponder. For example, you cannot keep fleeting thoughts from your mind any more than you can keep birds from flying over your head. However, you can prevent birds from building a nest on your head. True transformation requires that we keep any nest-building from occurring in our thoughts. We have the free will to look and think about whatever we choose. The way we exercise this free will is inextricably woven into our character. There is a nexus between our thoughts and our current reality. If we want to change our current reality, we must focus our eyes on something different and meditate on those new thoughts. We cannot think the same thoughts and expect different results.

In public administration, we must acknowledge that moral decisions affect the lives of people who work and live with us. The moral decisions we make at home and at work will affect our professional lives. The road to changing our destiny is a mere thought away. We have to accept the fact that our current state of affairs is directly attributable to character and habits we corporately exhibit. Those habits are composed of actions which originated within our thoughts. This is precisely what makes changing a corporate culture so difficult. No one person can change it all. It requires change on a much broader level.

Consistently making the "right" decisions, not just talking about making the right decisions, results in an invisible attribute with the power to influence others—moral authority.

Moral Authority

Moral authority is defined as a parallel congruence between one's beliefs and actions. When we have moral authority, we have influence and the power to make change happen. When moral authority is missing, we do not have the ability to influence others, nor do we have the power to make change. This is important, because moral authority is required to create an environment in which *integrity, accountability,* and *moral decision-making* can grow. Moral authority, then, functions as the first domino in a lineup. If it does not exist, the other dominos will not fall.

What would you think if Timothy Leary—a well-known proponent of the alleged benefits of LSD, an illegal drug—said, "Do not take illegal narcotics; they are bad for you"? You would probably respond by saying, "Who are you to lecture others about drugs?" How would you react if Jon Brower Minnoch, who, according to the *Guinness Book of Records,* was the world's heaviest person at 1,400 pounds, said, "A healthy diet and a good exercise routine are good for you"? You might say, "Who are you to lecture on healthy habits?"

The point is that people are not influenced by those who do not practice what they preach. People pay attention to whether your actions parallel your beliefs. If you talk the talk, you had better walk the walk—assuming you desire to make a difference with your life. Actions speak louder than words. In fact, people will remember *what you did* long after they have forgotten *what you said.*

Corporately speaking, in the context of public administration, moral authority means acting in alignment with your enabling legislation and fulfilling your statutorily required mandates. It means tracking your progress with objectively verifiable standards and reporting those activity measures on a regular basis. It means telling members of the legislative branch and executive branch the truth—not a watered-down version of the truth, but the truth as it appears in the morning before mascara and lipstick are applied.

Individually, moral authority means treating your employees equitably and serving the public faithfully. It means submitting to the authority of those in your chain of command. It means conducting audits and investigations with no preconceived expectations, following recognized standards, and reporting the results of those activities. It means silencing lies and misinformation by merely doing good and not retaliating. It means creating an environment at work in which employees will tell you the truth without fear of reprisal, and then rewarding those who do just that. It means accepting your responsibility as a leader to draw the line between "right" and "wrong" and clearly communicating the difference to your employees.

Conclusion

The question remains, how can we boost public trust? How do we as a country get back on track? Public trust is a necessity. It binds our democracy. Public trust naturally grows in an environment in which government leaders nurture integrity and accountability. Public trust will not grow when integrity and accountability are mere catchphrases that are not backed up by actions consistent with those precepts.

The often overlapping concepts of ethics, principles, and values are all component parts of morals. Within government, the morals we hold and the decisions we make pertaining to those morals will shape our future more than any other type of decision. In public administration, we can make moral decisions if we consistently rely on objective standards. Objective standards clearly differentiate right from wrong. Objective standards must also be employed to measure our progress, our production, and what we did with the resources we were allocated. Then we must communicate these objective standards in a manner the public can understand and by which it can hold government accountable.

Discussion Questions

1. What are the most important aspects of gaining the public trust?

2. Define and discuss accountability. What are some major elements of accountability? Why is this such an important ingredient for the successful manager?

3. What are objective standards and what are subjective standards? Is it important to have objective standards? Why?

4. What is personal integrity? How does character formation relate to personal integrity?

5. Define and discuss the concept of moral authority in the context of public administration. How important is it for a public administrator to understand this concept?

Notes

1. Gaillard Hunt, *The Writings of James Madison 1787-1790* (New York: G.P. Putnam's Sons, 1904).
2. Benson John Lossing, *A Biography of James A. Garfield* (New York: Henry S. Goodspeed & Co., 1882).
3. Philip Wheelwright, *A Critical Introduction to Ethics* (Whitefish, MT: Kessinger Publishing, LLC, 2005).
4. Ibid.
5. Ibid.

Recommended Resources

Denhardt, Robert B. *Public Administration: An Action Orientation.* Florence, KY: Cengage Learning, 2008.
Kaufman, George G. "Banking and Currency Crisis and Systemic Risk: Lessons from Recent Events." *Economic Perspectives* Q III (2000).

CHAPTER 10

Creating a Healthy Workplace Culture in Hard Times: Managing Workers through Deficits and Downturns in Austin, Texas

Toby Hammett Futrell

In less than ten years, our economy has produced two teeth-rattling recessions: the first beginning in 2002 after September 11, 2001, and then again in 2008. States, cities, counties, and school districts are trying to manage through record shortfalls while squeezed between soaring costs for health care and pensions and a growing opposition to tax increases. Though much has been written about the financial strategies for dealing with budget deficits, there has been little examination of how to manage—and, in fact, partner with—employees through the layoffs, freezes, and furloughs that accompany closing facilities and cutting services. Executing the science of organizational reductions and applying the art and heart of people management are very different efforts.

In a recession, employees are placed under enormous personal and professional stress. Long-established approaches to balancing a budget during a downturn leave government employees working harder—for less—with fewer resources, all while fearing the loss of their livelihood. During hard times, the brass ring for public managers is maintaining a workforce with high morale and organizational loyalty. This involves creating a working partnership between employees and management for dealing with the economic downturn. The success of such a partnership depends on strong two-way communication and allowing employees to become an integral part of the decision-making and organizational change that impact their jobs.

Backdrop

Austin, Texas, is the 15th largest city in the nation, having doubled in size approximately every 20 years since 1885. By the 1990s, Austin's economy was red hot. Extremely rapid growth in population and overall employment, combined with the maturation of the region's technology sector, created double-digit income growth. After Austin's phenomenal economic growth in the nineties, the fiscal decline at the beginning of the next decade hit the city particularly hard, proving that the higher you fly, the farther you can fall. The decline left Austin's recently passed general government budget, as well as the city's three-year financial forecast, deeply and structurally imbalanced. With a budget of $466 million and 5,047 employees, Austin was spending more than it was going to make.

To balance the fiscal year 2001-02 budget, the city initiated a hiring freeze and extensive cost-containment measures to cut expenditures by $34 million. In the following three years, Austin cut general fund expenditures an additional $89 million and eliminated 665 positions to achieve *structural balance*, meaning that ongoing expenditures matched ongoing revenue.

What Austin and other cities went through in the first half of this decade is again being played out in private- and public-sector organizations across the nation. Surveying a cross-section of U.S. employers in May 2009 showed that three-quarters of employers have taken at least one step to cut labor and operational costs in the past year. Sixty-four percent of those surveyed reported layoffs.

Cuts such as these represent a big challenge for public managers. Done wrong, reducing a budget deficit can leave a workforce disengaged, depressed, and angry. Done well, the end result is not just a balanced budget, but the retention of a motivated and loyal workforce that repositions an organization for a sustainable future.

It Starts at the Top

Fishing lore would have you believe that fish rot from the head down. I don't know if this is true of fish, but I do know that it is true in governmental downsizing. Managing the work environment, particularly during a recession, is a top-down job. Employees are looking up, watching management's every move, to gauge how they will be treated both during and after downsizing. An organization will fail or succeed based on how the top of the organization responds, and is perceived to respond, by employees. Don't underestimate a public manager's role in making sure a positive corporate culture emerges from the turmoil of downsizing. A healthy workplace culture can be built only from the top down in hard times.

The Three Cs

During a financial crisis, many managers automatically go into command and control mode, unintentionally treating their employees like children. Rather than fully engaging employees, they hold back information or dribble it out and sugarcoat it. Employees are cut out of decision-making. They are left on the sidelines, helplessly watching supervisors, human resources representatives, and lawyers scamper to one clandestine meeting after another. To survive a financial crisis with employee morale and productivity intact, it is critical for organizations to respect employees' dignity throughout the process. For a public manager, the "brass ring" is forging an effective partnership with employees. Austin successfully forged that partnership by paying attention to the three Cs: communication, control, and change.

Communication

In rough times, you can't communicate too much, but you can communicate unsuccessfully. Following conventional human resource and legal theory regarding conveying bad news to employees can lead to announcing personnel actions with little notice and making surprise layoffs. This is one of the biggest mistakes a public manager can make. Employee distrust and frustration will build with each new bombshell and dictum from on high. Contrary to conventional wisdom, managers should tell it all, tell it fast, and tell the truth. Communicating with respect requires a direct and honest dialogue with employees about the challenges and the choices the organization is facing.

To forge a true partnership with a workforce during hard times, you must communicate in a timely fashion and in a way that employees can believe in, relate to, and easily access. Keep employees in the loop. Start early and lay the groundwork with plain-English discussions about what is happening and what lies ahead. Create forums for two-way conversation, letting employees know management both wants and values their feedback and perspectives. Continue to communicate to build continued credibility. Above all, tell the truth. Although you want to convey a confident and can-do attitude, don't mislead employees or sugarcoat the situation.

Town Hall Meetings

Austin holds ongoing town hall meetings with employees at their worksites, scheduled on different days and times to make them accessible to all employees, regardless of when and where they work. This gives employees a chance to talk face-to-face with their city manager and department directors. All topics are on the table for discussion, uncensored and unscripted. As trends or themes develop during town hall meetings, they are noted, questions are answered, and information is communicated back to the entire workforce. Being prepared for tough questions in a town hall format is critical to success.

Rumor Control Hotline

The city created a Rumor Control Hotline using its intranet. Setting up a hotline can be as simple as establishing an email address for employees to use. Employees are encouraged to check the hotline site to obtain facts in response to rumors or hearsay circulating in their organization. Hotline responses to rumors need to be timely and truthful to be effective. Austin's management committed to providing frank responses within 48 hours. By serving as an early warning system, the hotline proved to be a simple, cost-effective way to reduce misinformation and eliminate destructive rumors in the workforce. Austin's hotline experiment made it clear that employees need not be kept in the dark to maintain organizational order. Employees can and will handle the truth if management listens and communicates in a genuine partnership with its workforce.

Employee Workforce Committee

Austin created an Employee Workforce Committee that meets monthly with the city manager. Employees nominate and elect their own departmental representatives. No managers are permitted to submit nominations or serve on the committee. Employee interest and participation is high; two-thirds of Austin's employees voted in the first election. The committee gives the city manager unfiltered feedback on workforce issues and attitudes, and it serves as another way to circulate information within the workforce.

Control

Bad decisions often accompany organizational downsizing. But this need not be the case. Managers *do* have choices in how they handle downsizing. So that employees are not relegated to the role of helpless victims, they must be allowed to take part in making the choices that will directly impact their lives and livelihoods. If workers are left on the sidelines, they will feel exploited by management. Fear, frustration, and anger build when employees feel powerless. Instead, management can empower employees, allowing them to retain some personal control, by including them as an integral part of the decision-making. When employees believe their involvement is both wanted and valued, they become part of the solution and are productive and engaged.

Listen to Employees and Act on Feedback

Employees have an invaluable perspective. Keeping employees informed, listening to their opinions, and then acting on that feedback is the single most important way to build a viable partnership with the workforce. When faced with a $38 million shortfall in fiscal year 2003-04, line employees in Austin identified $10.5 million in viable savings and cuts that management had not previously caught. Given a target and asked how to meet that target without layoffs, employees continued to propose creative solutions. One eight-person work unit, faced with the elimination of two positions, proposed reducing each of their 40-hour workweeks to a 30-hour workweek. The employees submitted a reduced work-hour proposal with a detailed work plan explaining how the employees could still accomplish their unit's mission through process reengineering. This plan produced savings equivalent to the cost of the two positions targeted for layoffs.

Employee Focus Groups and Straw Polls

Managers can use randomly selected employee focus groups and straw polls to help them make specific downsizing choices. Austin conducted an informal intranet poll of its employees on their preferences regarding a number of difficult decisions. For two years, more than 80 percent of the workforce voted to go without citywide pay increases to reduce the risk of employee layoffs. For these tools to be effective, results and an explanation of how management is going to use the results must be communicated back to the workforce.

Change

Government is change resistant. Recessions provide a rare opportunity for managers to sell needed change to their communities and councils and engage the workforce in true process improvements and reengineering.

Being empowered to effect meaningful change in their work processes will reenergize employees and foster organizational pride while reducing frustration. Making efficiency improvements, even while losing resources, is a way to reap gains in spite of the losses that come with downsizing.

Ask Employees

Employees know what needs to change. Ask them. In partnership with employees, Austin committed to rethinking and reshaping service delivery models before cutting direct service levels. Employees flowcharted more than 250 business processes to produce efficiencies and cost savings in areas such as development review and permitting, building inspections, project management, a consolidated call center, information technology, human resources, and purchasing. More than one-third of the total cuts made to structurally balance Austin's budget came from process improvements that reduced overhead and administrative costs to 4.5 percent of operations.

Celebrate Innovation

It is not uncommon to eliminate employee reward and recognition programs during a downturn. Don't. This is when you need them most. Never miss an opportunity to reward employees by simply recognizing a job well done. During the downturn, Austin used a number of different programs to celebrate passion and foster innovation in the workforce. Even when funds are tight, there are low-cost ways to motivate and recognize the contributions of the workforce. Something as simple as an on-the-spot recognition at an employee's work site, in front of his or her peers, can be very meaningful.

The End Result

Take care of employees by treating them with respect and dignity during a downsizing, and employees will, in turn, take care of the organization, its customers, and the community.

What does an organization gain by using the three Cs? Austin survived the downturn with minimal layoffs and a loyal, engaged workforce. Instead of losing employees as the economy rebounded, turnover was actually lowered from 9.1 percent to 7.5 percent, saving Austin an estimated $11 million in overtime, recruitment, and retraining costs. Austin's reputation as a stable employer helped the city not only retain top employee talent but ultimately remain competitive in attracting an educated workforce to its revitalized employment market.

What does the community gain? Austin employees increased their commitment to community service during the downturn, with 67 percent of the workforce volunteering in the community. For example, more than 400 employees volunteered during their lunch hour as mentors and tutors in Austin's low-performing schools during this time. And while Austin's Combined Charities Campaign has always been one of the strongest payroll contribution campaigns in Central Texas, employees actually increased their contributions doing the recession, even though they went without pay increases for several years.

Conclusion

A roller-coaster economy, coupled with the growing costs of pensions and health insurance, portends a future of cost pressures for the public sector. Learning how to manage a workforce through deficits and downturns will become a critical skill for public managers. Going beyond the science of organizational reductions and mastering the three Cs—communication, control, and change—will help public managers reposition their organizations for a sustainable future.

Discussion Questions

1. Identify and discuss some of the major elements a manager needs to know about how to operate in a cutback environment of fiscal stress.

2. Discuss some of the things the author did to create a working partnership between employees and management. Why was this partnership so important?

3. What were some of the measures that Austin, Texas, undertook to deal with the fiscal crisis of FY 01 and FY 02?

4. Identify and discuss wrong behaviors that managers often take when dealing with cutback management and fiscal stress. Why do these behaviors often backfire? What are some impacts of doing the wrong thing?

5. Discuss the three C process that was implemented in Austin. What important lessons can managers can learn from the three C process?

6. What value did town hall meetings have for the City Manager of Austin?

Recommended Resources

City of Austin Budget Office. *Budget Transmittal Letter.* Adopted budget, fiscal years 2002-03 through 2005-06.

CityTownInfo.com Staff. "Companies Cutting Back to Avoid Layoffs." CityTownInfo.com (April 13, 2009). http://www.citytowninfo.com/career-and-education-news/articles/companies-cutting-back-to-avoid-layoffs-09041301 (accessed November 24, 2009).

Downs, Alan. "Downsizing with Dignity." Business: The Ultimate Resource at About.com. http://humanresources.about.com/od/layoffsdownsizing/a/downsizing.htm (accessed October 19, 2009).

Frauenheim, Ed. "Flexible, But Too Quick to Lay Off?" Workforce Management, Global Work Watch blog (July 24, 2009). http://www.workforce.com/wpmu/globalwork/2009/07/24/flexible-but-too-quick-to-lay-off/ (accessed October 19, 2009).

Gotz, Jay. "Corporate Culture: How to Build an Effective One." *Fortune Small Business* (October 2009): 61.

Marks, Mitchell. *Charging Back Up the Hill: Workplace Recovery After Mergers, Acquisitions and Downsizing.* San Francisco: Jossey-Bass, 2003.

Osborne, David, and Hutchinson, Peter. *The Price of Government: Getting the Results We Need in an Age of Permanent Fiscal Crisis.* St. Paul: The Public Strategies Group, Inc., 2004.

Robinson, Ryan. "City of Austin Demographic Data." City of Austin Planning Department: July 2006.

Stellman, Leslie Robert. *Mandatory Legal Considerations for Counties that are Considering Furloughs, Layoff, Benefits Reductions and/or Salary Freezes.* Towson, MD: Hodes, Pessin & Katz, PA, 2009.

Sunnucks, Mike. "Layoffs, Furloughs, Pay Cuts Can Result in Lawsuits." *Phoenix Business Journal* (May 15, 2009).

CHAPTER 11

Maximizing Public Organization Talent Strategically and Systemically

Anthony Bingham

People—their knowledge, skills, and abilities—are a primary focus for most senior leaders today because of people's unique ability to help organizations succeed. No longer are systems and processes the differentiators for organizations; these are becoming commodities. Today, in the knowledge economy, people are *the* differential advantage when it comes to organizational performance. Government agencies, just like private-sector firms, must be strategic about managing and leveraging their talent for maximum results.

Skills Gap

At the same time, there is a growing skills gap in the workforce. Organizational leaders point out that their number-one concern is finding the right people to fill a growing list of vacant positions—a list that has only grown longer during the economic crisis that began in 2008.

The American Society for Training and Development (ASTD) defines a *skills gap* as a significant difference between an organization's skill needs and the current capabilities of its workforce. It is the point at which it is very difficult to achieve strategic goals because the right employees with the right skills are not in the right positions at the right time.

There are many reasons for the skills gap in addition to the state of the U.S. economy. Some estimates predict that as many as 60 percent of federal workers will be eligible to retire over the next decade. At the same time, federal jobs, which account for about 2 percent of the U.S. workforce, are multiplying under the Obama administration. And, while retirement has been postponed by many federal employees because of the economy, the federal government still faces many challenges in filling its leadership pipeline. A U.S. Office of Personnel Management (OPM) Federal Human Capital Survey, administered to more than 210,000 federal workers in 2008, showed that only 42 percent are satisfied with the policies and practices of the senior leaders of their agencies.

Adding to the skills gap is the fact that jobs are changing. Many require higher levels of technical or professional skill than in the past, while educational attainment lags the need for these skills. A study by the National Center on Education and the Economy projected that by 2020, the U.S. economy will be short several million workers with at least some college experience.

Four Key Skill Areas

In a white paper, *Bridging the Skills Gap*, ASTD reported four key areas in which skills are the most lacking:

- **Basic skills**—the three Rs (reading, writing, and arithmetic), customer service, communications, and business acumen

- **Technical and professional skills**

- **Management and leadership skills** such as supervision, team leadership, goal setting, planning, motivation, decision-making, and ethical judgment

- **Emotional intelligence.**

For decades, organizations have developed employees' skills through traditional practices such as succession planning, mentoring, coaching, and training. Now there is increasing pressure for better performance and less time to achieve results, and these old practices are being called into question. Organizations find that they cannot muster the talent they need when they need it to achieve their goals.

It is not just individual organizations or sectors that are suffering from the skills gap. Communities, states, regions, and entire nations pay a heavy price when they cannot find or equip workers with the right skills for critical jobs.

Workforce Composition

The composition of the workforce itself is changing in ways we have never experienced and for which many institutions are unprepared. According to the Bureau of Labor Statistics (BLS), the size of the workforce in the United States in 2014 will be roughly 162 million. Estimates suggest that the Net Generation, one name for the youngest generation of workers, for whom the Internet is as much a part of their lives as the air they breathe, will make up 47 percent of the workforce in 2014.

Stereotypes of the Net Gens—they can't make a decision, they don't want to "pay their dues," they ignore hours and dress codes, and they expect constant feedback—strike fear in the hearts of many managers. But Don Tapscott, a consultant on organizational transformation, writes in his book *Grown Up Digital*, "The evidence is strong that Net Gens are the smartest generation ever. Raw IQ scores are climbing by three points a decade since World War II, and they have been increasing across racial, income, and regional boundaries."

Tapscott adds: "As employees and managers, the Net Generation is approaching work collaboratively, collapsing the rigid hierarchy, and forcing organizations to rethink how they recruit, compensate, develop, and supervise talent." Meanwhile, the large-scale retirement of baby boomers has not happened as expected, making some succession plans obsolete.

Integrated Talent Management

In reality, organizations will always experience a skills gap if they are staying ahead of shifting conditions in their environment and the changing expectations of their constituents. The key to achieving success under these circumstances is to have systems and processes in place to connect talent to strategy and goals. Achieving such a balance between workforce and mission makes it more challenging than ever to equip organizations with the skills they need in an increasingly global, virtual, and changing world—which must be done faster, with fewer resources.

These days, it is not enough to simply hire smart people and develop their knowledge and skills. The organization must fully understand its employees' capabilities and ensure that they are applied to maximum effect. With a change in the presidential administration and new challenges on the horizon, now is the time for agencies to be strategic about finding, developing, engaging, and retaining key talent. This is a time for organizations' learning function to become more efficient and effective, taking a leading role in managing talent and linking it to strategic organizational goals.

ASTD recommends an integrated approach to managing talent in an organization. Integrated talent management strategically unites all human capital functions to maximize organizational effectiveness. Such an approach integrates the processes for acquisition, recruiting, and development into one effort with a common goal: a workforce capable of optimal performance.

Eight Recommended Strategies and Tactics

An ASTD/i4cp (Institute for Corporate Productivity) study examined a diverse group of organizations to discern the best practices of effective talent management programs. Following are the talent management strategies and tactics most strongly associated with success, as well as recommendations for organizations interested in improving their talent management programs and systems:

- Drive talent management from the top of the organization to ensure that senior management supports it and to prevent the work from falling into silos.

- Ensure that talent management efforts support key agency strategies.

- Align all components of talent management to support optimal performance.

- Manage talent management with a long-range perspective but with the ability to respond to changes in capability requirements as needed.

- Keep the emphasis on talent, through good times and bad.

- Nurture a talent-oriented culture.

- Use talent-management metrics.

- Cultivate the skills needed to manage talent effectively.

Lessons from the Economic Crisis

Few industries are immune to the effects of the global recession that began in 2008, and few anticipated the breadth and depth of the economic crisis. Unprepared, many companies in trouble reacted from the gut, cutting their workforce first and realizing too late that their competitive advantage—their top talent—had walked out the door.

Organizations that have been shaken but not brought down by the economic crisis are those that already understood the value of their human capital. A study by ASTD and i4cp, *Learning in Tough Economic Times*, shows that 38 percent of companies surveyed are placing more emphasis on learning during this economic downturn. When the time came for belt tightening, they already knew what capabilities they needed to be more productive, innovative, and goal-focused. And they had processes in place to find, hire, assign, and keep the talent they needed most.

These organizations responded quickly by taking actions such as leveraging technology to design, deliver, and account for employee learning and development. Those responsible for employee development didn't hesitate to move training out of the classroom and to pare down training content to the essentials to achieve increased efficiency and effectiveness. They ensured that every learning program, however small, supported a key goal in some way—or it didn't survive.

Leadership

One of the toughest challenges of the current economic crisis is that leaders must act even when they don't know what is coming next or how long recovery will take. But one fact is certain: old ways of doing things are not coming back. This is especially true in the public sector. The Obama administration is asking federal agencies to undertake meaningful change and strengthen their performance. What leadership practices will be most effective for such an undertaking?

Booz Allen Hamilton, collaborating with Steve Kelman, a professor of public management at Harvard's Kennedy School of Government, gathered evidence about the success and failures of government executives who tried to bring change to their agencies. The resulting study, called *What It Takes to Change Government,* was released in July 2009.

Six Leadership Best Practices

Among the lessons learned about the practices of leaders at successful agencies were:

- Pursue just two or three goals.
- Get a running start by being proactive.
- Use a strategic planning process, but don't overdo it.
- Manage within the organization, not just at 50,000 feet.
- Use performance measures.
- Consider reorganizing, even if there is resistance.

One surprising finding, according to the report's authors, was that many agencies ignored basic management practices. For example, all federal agencies are required by law to have performance metrics, but not all agencies use them. In this study, only the managers who used metrics worked at the successful agencies, including the U.S. Government Accountability Office (GAO) and the Internal Revenue Service (IRS).

The Impact of Web 2.0

Managers, learning leaders, and human capital officers face one additional and significant factor in transforming their organizations into learning organizations and managing their talent for maximum effectiveness: Web 2.0 technologies. These technologies and tools, especially those that enable employees to collaborate, connect, and learn informally, will be a major force for change in all types of organizations.

While most institutions have become very adept at providing formal learning and remain relatively committed to employee development regardless of the economic or political cycle, the majority of learning at work today is informal and often occurs outside the purview of managers or training professionals. On their own, using familiar Web.2.0 tools such as wikis, blogs, and social networking software, employees have embraced informal peer-to-peer knowledge sharing.

ASTD's research team completed a study in early 2009 to understand how training and development professionals were employing Web 2.0 to provide learning tools in their workplaces. The study found that the vast potential of Web 2.0 technologies has not been realized by most organizations' learning functions. And while many are still becoming familiar with these technologies, the majority of respondents believe that their learning functions will use Web 2.0 technologies more during the next three years.

Why are organizations adopting these technologies? The most widely reported reason—cited by 77 percent of the respondents—was to improve knowledge sharing. The second most widely cited reason was to foster learning in the organization.

When looking at how to boost adoption of Web 2.0, ASTD's study found that middle managers are most likely to be responsible for introducing Web 2.0 technologies into the organization. Younger workers are more likely to use Web 2.0 applications on the job, whether management wants them to or not, according to a 2008 Symantec survey. Informal learning and networking with Web 2.0 technologies has a strong grassroots component, as employees deploy tools they already use for non-work activities to get around roadblocks to collaboration and just-in-time learning in their organizations.

Six Web 2.0 Best Practices

Based on ASTD's research, three strategies will increase the likelihood of success in creating an effective learning function with Web 2.0: increased investment in learning-related Web 2.0, encouraging wide participation in using these technologies for learning, and gaining top-level support for their use. Here are six best practices for implementing Web 2.0 technologies:

- Perform sufficient advanced planning before rolling out a new technology.

- Train employees in using the tools, and communicate how they should be used.

- Build controls to ensure integrity of content, processes, and measurements.

- Don't control usage so much that it prevents participation and erodes trust.

- Allow enough time for the new technologies to take root.

- Secure senior-level commitment.

Together, managers and learning professionals can drive adoption of this game-changing technology and quantifiably demonstrate its effectiveness.

Unprecedented Opportunities

As conventional wisdom tells us, exceptional challenges can open up exceptional opportunities. The skills gap, the economic crisis, and the power of Web 2.0 will force change on the public and private sectors, ready or not.

Seven Key Human Capital Steps

The current challenges have pushed human capital to the forefront in many government agencies. Chief human capital officers and senior learning professionals have an opportunity to demonstrate their value as never before by taking these steps:

- Invest in employee development and commit resources to learning initiatives that support goals and strategies.

- Create an environment of continuous learning and provide appropriate learning and development opportunities.

- Benchmark organization-wide learning against best practices.

- Recognize and reward learning and development that supports current and future skill needs.

- Integrate human capital functions and processes to manage talent strategically.

- Take action to identify and close the skills gap.

- Engage senior leadership as teachers, mentors, and champions.

These challenges present a unique opportunity for public managers and leaders in employee training and development to develop a highly knowledgeable, skilled workforce capable of delivering exceptional public service and helping private-sector organizations compete in the global economy. There has never been a more important time to leverage talent and unite all human capital management functions to maximize organizational effectiveness.

Results of the 2008 Federal Human Capital Survey[1]

According to the executive summary of the 2008 Federal Human Capital Survey (FHCS), the survey "focuses on employee perceptions regarding critical areas of their work life, areas which drive employee satisfaction, commitment, and ultimately retention in the workforce." The survey, to which more than 210,000 federal employees responded, paints a picture of steady progress but shows there is still much work to be done, especially with regard to the talent pipeline.

The FCHS measures four indices: leadership and knowledge, results-oriented performance culture, talent management, and job satisfaction. The 2008 results showed small increases in all four indices, with job satisfaction rated highest. Respondents gave government agencies' ability to bring in and retain talent moderate ratings. Only 44.9 percent of respondents agreed that their work unit is able to recruit people with the right skills. The lowest ratings were given to government agencies' ability to create a culture that "instills a results orientation and rewards employees for performance." Less than one-third (31.4 percent) of the government workforce believes differences in performance are recognized in a meaningful way, and only 39 percent say they are satisfied with their opportunity to get a better job in their organization.

The Nuclear Regulatory Commission Ranks First in the Best Places to Work in the Federal Government[2]

For the second time, the Nuclear Regulatory Commission (NRC) was rated by its employees the best place to work in the federal government. The Best Places to Work[3] index provides an assessment of employee satisfaction and commitment in federal agencies. The rankings are based on the U.S. Office of Personnel Management's (OPM) 2008 Federal Human Capital Survey, which has been administered every two years since 2002. It is particularly noteworthy that both the NRC and the U.S. Government Accountability Office were ranked first and second, respectively, in 2007 and significantly improved their scores in the 2009 index to maintain their high rankings.

NRC employees mention that challenging and interesting work, access to training courses and professional development programs, and a focus on work-life balance are some of the reasons they enjoy working at the NRC.

Discussion Questions

1. What is the skills gap facing government today?

2. How is the workforce composition changing and how might this affect government's talent management needs and strategic thinking?

3. What talent management strategies and tactics should public organizations consider to meet their skills gap requirements and respond to changing workforce realities?

4. What leadership practices will be most effective?

5. How is Web 2.0 a double-edged sword?

Notes

1. U.S. Office of Personnel Management, "2008 Federal Human Capital Survey," (Washington, D.C., 2008), http://www.fhcs.opm. gov/2008FILES/2008_Govtwide_Report.pdf (accessed September 18, 2009).
2. Nuclear Regulatory Commission, "Making Our Mission Yours," 2008, http://video.nrc.gov/Player.aspx?Event=376 (accessed September 18, 2009).
3. The Best Places to Work in the Federal Government rankings are produced by the Partnership for Public Service and American University's Institute for the Study of Public Policy Implementation (ISPPI). More information can be found at www.bestplacestowork.org.

Recommended Resources

American Society for Training and Development. "Bridging the Skills Gap." (white paper, Alexandria, VA, 2006).

American Society for Training and Development. "Learning in Tough Economic Times: How Corporate Learning is Meeting the Challenges." (research study, Alexandria, VA, 2009).

American Society for Training and Development. "Transforming Learning with Web 2.0 Technologies." (research study, Alexandria, VA, 2009).

American Society for Training and Development and Institute for Corporate Productivity. "Talent Management Practices and Opportunities." (research study, Alexandria, VA, 2009).

Mader, Dave, Jeff Myers, and Steven Kelman. "What it Takes to Change Government: Successfully Executing Ambitious Strategies in Government." Booz Allen Hamilton, 2009. http://www.boozallen.com/media/file/what-it-takes-change-gov-viewpoint.pdf (accessed September 18, 2009).

Tapscott, Don. *Grown Up Digital: How the Net Generation is Changing Your World.* New York: McGraw-Hill, 2009.

U.S. Office of Personnel Management. "2008 Federal Human Capital Survey." Washington, D.C., 2008. http://www.fhcs.opm.gov/2008FILES/2008_Govtwide_Report.pdf (accessed September 18, 2009).

PART 4

Strategic Knowledge and Technology Management

CHAPTER 12

Technology Challenges for 21st-Century Government

Alan P. Balutis

Consider how the world has changed in the last 25 to 30 years, since the Reagan administration's Grace Commission investigated federal government waste and inefficiency and the Reform 88 initiative, intended to improve management of the government, was launched. The first microcomputers were just being introduced, and personal computers were mostly the realm of hobbyists. People came to work at central offices. A major role of the U.S. General Services Administration (GSA) was to manage the building of, or build themselves, a multitude of federal buildings and offices to house all those workers. Most businesses were local or within driving distance. Mobile telephones existed only as car phones for the well-to-do. Telework was largely unknown. Research was conducted using books and at libraries.

Contrast this with the world we live in now—what the Gartner Group, an IT consulting firm, calls Future Worker 2015. Long-distance travel is common. Personal computers and cell phones are ubiquitous. Telework is routine. Business partners are as likely to be on different continents as in different cities. Research reports include graphics, sounds, and multimedia gathered in minutes on the web or through electronic interactions.

The Obama administration is considering building on and expanding existing e-government initiatives, increasing government's openness and transparency, making use of so-called Web 2.0 collaborative tools, and exploring cloud computing (network access to a shared pool of computing resources) and other mechanisms to reduce existing infrastructure investments. Moreover, technology is being viewed as an enabler in dealing with major challenges in such policy arenas as health, transportation, energy, and the environment.

Technology Trends: Short Term

In the *Analytical Perspectives* volume of the *FY 2010 Budget of the United States Government,* the new president outlined a management and performance agenda. That agenda is organized around the following themes:

- Putting performance first by replacing the Bush-era Performance Assessment Rating Tool (PART) with a new performance improvement and analysis framework

- Ensuring responsible spending of Recovery Act funds

- Transforming the federal workforce by reforming the current hiring process and hiring several hundred thousand civilian employees during the next four years

- Managing across sectors (e.g., private and nonprofit) and collaborating across levels of government

- Reforming federal contracting and acquisition

- Enhancing transparency, technology, and participatory democracy.

At the time this chapter was written, only the initial thinking about such a management and technology agenda is available. Here are some early plans and changes:

- Departments and agencies will harness new technologies to publish information about their operations and decisions online, in ways that are readily available to the public.

- The administration will provide more transparency and openness and devise new tools to let citizens participate and have their voices heard.

- How will federal officials manage millions of public comments in a meaningful way? Automation is the answer, observers say. Business intelligence software, including data mining, decision support, and reporting and web analytic tools, will help agencies extract useful information from public comments.

- Government must manage its information technology programs efficiently while reducing redundancy and risk from outdated and interoperable computer systems.

- The shift to cloud computing is inevitable.

- Web 2.0—social networking tools—is part of the next wave of government technology adoption.

- For 21st-century governments, human resource and management policies could become a differentiator in those governments' ability to attract the best workers (regardless of where these workers live and the times of day they work). These policies should support workers' expectations that the same productivity, multitasking, and mobility tools with which they grew up should also be in the workplace.

- Government agencies should adopt the collaborative open-source software model.

- The Recovery Act includes a robust ($7.2 billion) broadband stimulus program intended to spur deployment of high-speed Internet connectivity to areas with limited or no service.

- The president has appointed the country's first federal chief technology officer (CTO).

- Information technology investments that reduce energy should get a boost in this administration as we seek to "green" IT.

- IT security and privacy remain high-profile areas of concern. The Commission on Cybersecurity for the 44th Presidency, a bipartisan effort on the part of computer security experts, has recently recommended that President Barack Obama set up a high-level post to increase IT security and counter cybercrime, citing intrusions within the computer systems at the Departments of Defense, State, Homeland Security, and Commerce.

Challenges lie ahead for this ambitious technology agenda. They include the federal government's organizational structure, the inability of managers to understand how these new technology tools create value, and executives who are suspicious of or uncomfortable with perceived changes or risks. How the administration manages and copes with these government cultural barriers will determine success (or failure) much more than will any technological challenges.

Technology Trends: Longer Term

A recent *Wall Street Journal* special report, "Thinking about Tomorrow," begins as follows:

> Let's get this out of the way first—in the next ten years, no one will travel to work by jet pack or have robot maids that serve dinner. But technology will continue to transform the rituals of everyday life—sometimes in startling ways.

Technology will continue to bring about major changes in government and in governance, just as it did in the 20th century. We should acknowledge that it's been far easier to project technology trends than it has been to predict which ones will really take hold and what their effects will be on government and society.

The existing technology landscape for our new president in 2009—limited telework efforts, parallel processing, data mining/warehousing, business intelligence software, mobile computing, and so on—will change in his first and (potentially) second term. In its place, the nation's leaders will encounter new strategic information and communication technologies that will change government: government 2.0, green IT, distributed co-creation, ubiquitous bandwidth, virtual space and simulation, smart environments, and the like.

Many of these changes have been outlined recently by Cisco Systems' futurist, Dave Evans (see Figure 12-1).

Figure 12-1: Near-Term Technology Trends

BUSINESS	TECHNOLOGY	SOCIETAL

Sensor mesh networks · Human augmentation

More than 10 years until adoption

Mobile robots · Tera-architectures · Radical healthcare innovation

Behavioral economics · RFID · 3D printing · Virtual worlds

5–10 years until adoption · Web platforms · Social software · SaaS/alternate delivery models · Proliferation of education delivery methods

Collective intelligence

IT industry collision · Enterprise information management · Virtualization 2.0 · Pervasive video

2–5 years until adoption · Service-oriented architecture · Empowered entrepreneurship

Globalized microbusiness · Unified communications and collaboration · Web 2.0 workspace technologies · Green IT · Retirement of baby boomers

Enterprise mobility

Business interaction optimization · Web 2.0 business models · Digitization · Open platform · Privacy

Rise of emerging economies · *Less than 2 years until adoption* · Mashups and co-creation · Consumerization · Rise of the millennials

Voice/data convergence

Source: Cisco Systems, 2009. Reprinted with permission.

But what trends are we seeing that have the greatest potential to affect government, governance, and politics in our society? In his provocative podcast *The Technology Avalanche*, Evans outlines a (very) brief history of human innovation. He notes that these technological developments—from the first locomotive to human genome mapping—have taken place during less than 0.2 percent of the time humans have existed. But those innovations were nothing! All of them will be dwarfed in the next few years by accelerating, exponential technology growth unlike anything before—a technology avalanche. Evans goes on to forecast explosive growth in the four pillars of technology:

- **Storage.** In 20 years, for a little over $100, a computer user could purchase 11 petabytes (11 million gigabytes) of storage.

- **Bandwidth** and **computing.** The first quantum computers are expected to be available around 2020. By the same time, a $1,000 personal computer will have the raw processing power of the human brain.

- **Information.** In 2015, the U.S. Internet will be at least 50 times larger than it was in 2006.

What changes does Evans see from these trends? First, all technological tools will be connected, and the Internet will be accessible through countless new devices. Wireless communication will be everywhere, and your phone will be your computer. And, beyond that, we will begin to get close to traveling to work by jet pack or teleporter and having robots that not only serve dinner but replace humans in the workforce.

Other Changing Horizons

What do other forecasters predict? Computer Sciences Corporation's (CSC) Leading Edge Forum just issued a report called *Digital Disruptions*, noting seven disruptions that already are influencing or will influence business, society, and government in the 21st century. The list includes:

- New media

- Virtual reality

- Social media and networks

- Information transparency

- Communications infrastructure

- Next-generation computational power

- User-machine interfaces.

The CSC team considered including a number of other technologies on the list before settling on these final seven. Among those considered were collaborative technologies and cloud computing. They chose not to single out collaborative technologies because they are integral to a number of the items that made the list. And cloud computing is very much with us today, ever since Google, Inc., CEO Eric Schmidt uttered the term in 2006.

On another front, the federal government will face a retirement tsunami in its workforce. According to many experts, 60 percent of the government's top managers will be eligible to retire in the next decade. The U.S. Office of Personnel Management has projected that the number of retirements will peak between 2008 and 2010—just as President Obama is launching his new administration. Over the next five years, the federal government could lose more than 550,000 employees.

The Chinese write the word *crisis* with two characters, one of which means *danger* and the other *opportunity*. The pending workforce crisis (the retirement tsunami) can also be viewed as a tremendous opportunity—to reshape the federal government, flatten hierarchies, remake the way government and citizens interact, and change the culture of the bureaucracy. It is an opportunity to mold government into a high-performance organization, create a more resilient workforce, and make government itself more resilient. It is an opportunity to build a 21st century government and workforce. This kind of opportunity has not come along since the Hoover Commission government efficiency studies were issued in the 1940s and 1950s and is not likely to be available again for another generation.

Technology has enabled the development of revolutionary business models for government and has elevated citizen and customer expectations. Secure communications are available anywhere and at any time through broadband and wireless. The network phenomenon has changed when, where, and how we collaborate and transact business. Rich and social media concepts, including video anywhere, instant messaging and presence awareness, podcasts, wikis, blogs, and shared bookmarks, have changed transactions and how we communicate. Governments must now change their business models from those of the last 50 or more years to those that will characterize the 21st century and beyond.

Discussion Questions

1. What are some early signs of the Obama administration's management and technology agenda?

2. What are some of the longer-term trends and challenges, including the four pillars of technology?

3. What new opportunities do these technology changes offer for 21st-century government?

Recommended Resources

Leading Edge Forum. "Digital Disruptions: Technology Innovations Powering 21st-Century Business." Computer Sciences Corporation, 2009. http://assets1.csc.com/lef/downloads/LEF_2008DigitalDisruptions.pdf (accessed September 18, 2009).

Evans, Dave. "The Technology Avalanche." Cisco, 2009. http://newsroom.cisco.com/dlls/podcasts/ciscocast_dave_evans_060407.html (accessed September 18, 2009).

Morello, Diane, and Betsy Burton. "Future Worker 2015: Extreme Individualization." Gartner Group, 2006. http://www.gartner.com/DisplayDocument?doc_cd=138172 (accessed September 18, 2009).

U.S. Office of Management and Budget. "Analytical Perspectives in Budget of the United States Government FY 2010." Washington, D.C., 2009.

Journal Reports. "Thinking about Tomorrow." *Wall Street Journal*, January 28, 2008, Special Report.

CHAPTER 13

Webcentricity and Five Challenges for Public Management

Alan R. Shark

Social networking is gaining more attention, thanks to an ever-expanding array of fascinating and useful applications. We seem to have moved from the information age to the interactive or connected age in relatively short order, in spite of any perceived disadvantages of being constantly connected. It was one thing to have our electronic gadgets and devices always on, but it did not take long for many of us to find *ourselves* increasingly "always on" too. Emails and text messages beg for immediate responses. This chips away at the traditional 9-to-5 workday, weekends-away-from-work mentality. More often than not, work is intertwined into our daily lives 24/7, just like our devices.

Public managers are challenged as never before to expose themselves to an uncertain yet demanding public. The challenge ahead is not only to figure out how best to embrace the new webcentricity in one's personal life, but also to figure out the enormous power, pitfalls, and possibilities of webcentricity that can be integrated into professional life. For government applications, much time must be devoted to planning as well as experimentation, exploration, and careful navigation. What follows are five webcentric trends that public managers simply cannot ignore.

The Pocket Computer/Phone

In 2007, Apple Computer dazzled the world with its iPhone. Not only did the phone have hundreds of clever and functional features, it was the first successful foray into the cell phone market by a *computer* manufacturer. The iPhone's features raised the bar for all technology manufacturers, but now most other computer manufacturers are rushing to develop new and better smartphones in an attempt to outperform the iPhone.

Meanwhile, the projected growth rate of smartphone users is staggering, and the explosion of new interactive applications continues. Many people expected that the smartphone and the computer would converge—it was only a matter of time—but it's occurring more quickly than anyone imagined. A trip to the online Apple store reveals thousands of new and dynamic applications, many of which are free or inexpensive, but few have anything to do with actually making or receiving telephone calls. Cell phones (and laptops, notebooks, and netbooks) have morphed into computers, and computers have morphed into cell phones. These devices merge voice, data, and video, allowing people around the world to see and hear things instantly and differently.

According to the Pew Internet and American Life Project, 62 percent of all Americans use wireless, mobile devices. A growing number of citizens now read news on a small screen, be it handheld or computer. No wonder print newspapers and magazines are struggling and going out of business in record numbers, as advertisers go where the customers are. The millennial generation gets most, if not all, of its news from handheld devices or computers. Many millennials do not own landline phones. They use cell phones instead of wristwatches and alarm clocks. They use handhelds or laptops to watch "traditional" TV programs, movies, and videos and have little need for an actual TV.

For everyone serving in the field of public administration, there is no escaping the changes in technology and how they are being embraced and adopted by citizens. Public managers must examine how people are processing news and information in this new connected society.

Each age grouping appears to process information differently, but people of all ages are moving rapidly into cyberspace, even if only to send email or get directions. (Seventy-eight percent of adults over 64 years old use the Internet primarily for sending and receiving emails.) According to the Pew Internet and American Life Project, some 55 percent of all adult Americans now have a high-speed Internet connection at home, and nearly one-third of broadband users pay more to get faster connections. Pew also reports that 75 percent of 18- to 24-year-olds have a presence on a social networking site, as do 57 percent of adults 25 to 34 years old and 19 percent of 45- to 54-year-olds. Social networking's popularity is growing among all age groups. In this connected society, we must take into account a new paradigm for managing public expectations.

Transparency and Citizen Engagement

President Barack Obama, the nation's first technology president, ran for the nation's highest office on a platform of changing government by making it more open and transparent, while encouraging greater citizen engagement and empowerment, mostly through web-based technology. One of his first initiatives was to ask all federal agencies to establish procedures to carry out this new mandate. The Economic Recovery and Reinvestment Act of 2009 requires each of the 50 states to post information on its website showing how funds are being spent and to solicit and share citizen feedback. States are also required to update their sites with spending progress reports on a regular basis.

Many state and local governments are also changing how they disclose information and encourage participation. However, not all public managers and elected leaders have warmly embraced such initiatives. Many think that these initiatives will expose what some citizens may consider wasteful spending and bloated bureaucratic organizations.

On the other hand, many enlightened public managers believe transparency and citizen engagement will strengthen their relationships with citizens and residents. They know what when knowledge is used properly, citizens benefit.

Web 2.0 to 3.0: The Social Networking Phenomenon

The terms *Web 2.0* and *3.0* refer to the new kinds of applications and opportunities available online. *Web 2.0* generally connotes web-based applications such as second-generation social networking sites, wikis, new communication tools, collaborative or social tagging, intelligent interfaces with mobile Internet devices and cameras, blogs, and text messaging. *Web 3.0* describes the evolution of the "intelligent web," where we will find micro-formats, natural language search capability, data-mining, machine learning, recommendation agents, and artificial intelligence technologies.

The 3.0 web browser will be far more intuitive; it will know what people most often like to do or search for—and so much more. Moreover, because the same technology will be available on mobile devices, futuristic scenes in movies such as *Mission Impossible,* in which actor Tom Cruise walks through a shopping area as hidden biometric scanning identifies him and every store he passes offers him deals by name and preference, will not seem so far-fetched.

Twitter

Twitter, an incredibly fast-growing social networking site that boasts 200 million unique users as of this writing, has become the nation's "chat box" for everyone from rock stars to sports and news junkies—and even governments. Users can update their Twitter accounts from computers or mobile devices—anywhere there is a broadband connection. In what some refer to as *microblogging,* people "tweet" snippets from their everyday lives. At the same time, local governments are offering real-time notifications of crimes being committed, fires and other emergencies, road work and accidents, and weather alerts, as well as notices about meetings and other events. Local governments also are encouraging citizens to report happenings via Twitter.

One of a growing number of social networking utilities linking people with common interests, *blogs*—informal online journals—also are used as a tool for expressing feelings, voicing opinions, or sharing a political point of view. Blog entries can include videos or photos.

YouTube

YouTube has become the nation's repository for home and professional short videos. Thousands of new videos are posted every hour, 24 hours a day. Less well known are contributions from numerous federal, state, and local agencies, which include informational videos about health alerts and issues, transportation, training, recruiting, and local attractions; messages from elected leaders; and tutorials.

The ability to share visual media can be very empowering. At least one enterprising politician encourages his citizens to post videos or still pictures of problems, such as potholes, broken streetlights, or improperly picked-up trash, that they used to write or call about. Meanwhile, the ubiquity of digital cameras and cell phone or smartphone cameras has even helped citizens act as eyewitnesses to crime. Perhaps technology has taken the old neighborhood watch concept to a new level.

Governmental Social Networking Sites

Federal, state, and local governments are experimenting with many other social networking sites, such as Facebook and MySpace. GovLoop.com, a social networking site for government leaders at all levels, boasts over 10,000 users; 80 percent of that growth occurred in one year. A highly resourceful group called MuniGov2.0 (https://sites.google.com/site/munigov20) has over 400 members (membership is free) who meet regularly (virtually, of course) to explore how Web 2.0 can be used to improve citizen services and communication. And, through the popular virtual world website Second Life, the U.S. Department of Commerce's National Oceanic and Atmospheric Administration (NOAA) offers an amazing application: two virtual islands that students (and adults) can visit to experience what NOAA does in a highly experiential and interactive way.

In addition to participating in the social networking trend, major universities are offering online classes, cities and counties are creating virtual experiences to reach out to citizens, and federal agencies have storefronts for recruiting specialized staff.

The Dangers of Social Viral Media

The immediacy of the online world creates both pitfalls and opportunities. During the swine flu pandemic scare in 2009, one information-gathering group counted 10,000 Twitter "tweets" on the topic per hour. Most of these were anecdotal observations, opinions, and downright false information. Online, information and media are frequently wrong. Public administrators are facing a new challenge: monitoring what is being said and broadcast throughout a community—or the entire connected world! Falsely screaming "fire" in one country could start a digital stampede elsewhere.

Not too long ago, a clever marketer posted three low-cost videos on YouTube that showed young people popping popcorn just by placing a few cell phones in front of a handful of corn kernels. When the phones rang, the popcorn exploded. The young actors appeared genuinely stunned. The not-so-subliminal message was that if cell phones could generate enough radiation to heat a kernel of corn, just think what that radiation could be doing to your brain each time you hold a cell phone to your ear. More than 30 million people across the globe were baffled by the videos. They were part of a marketing hoax that was perpetuated for many days before the plot and strategy were exposed. The marketer gained millions of dollars worth of free advertising for Bluetooth headsets, which enable the use of cell phones without having to hold the phone to the ear. This serves as a prime example of how viral messages or video can spin almost out of control into a very believing universe.

The Immediacy of Video

Budget woes always bring about innovations intended to save money. However, even before the recession that began in late 2007, advances in technology were making peer-to-peer videoconferencing a preferred method for instant meetings. High-definition (HD) video and sound can almost make it seem as if people in disparate locations are all in the same room. The next generation of video cameras will be smaller, lighter, and more powerful in every way. New still cameras can take HD video and can easily be connected to the Internet and big-screen TVs. These cameras will enable even more peer-to-peer and group-to-group communications. And the new easy-to-use video processor programs allow almost anyone to produce movies.

What are the implications of high-quality video for government? Public safety communication officers are beginning to think about new training for their dispatchers, who will soon be able to see emergencies from the field in real time and in HD. They are concerned that many dispatchers may be unprepared for the potential shock of seeing blood and trauma in ways that could be disturbing, shocking, and far more stressful than answering emergency telephone calls.

Meanwhile, the news media is encouraging ordinary people to be citizen reporters by taking and uploading video of news events. Often the first people to arrive at a scene are amateurs clicking and posting away long before anyone from the media arrives. Clearly, this increase in "unplanned" transparency will create new demands (and opportunities for teachable moments) to which the public sector will need to respond.

Managing E-Connectivity

Government leaders are realizing that the idea of "e-government" is being replaced by the reality of our connected society—e-connectivity. Among other challenges, governments must recognize that the new social networking technologies put their technology infrastructure at greater risk for malicious attacks and breaches in security than ever before. Despite these concerns, thousands of local, state, and federal enterprises are already experimenting with social networks and Web 2.0 applications. While all the focus thus far has been on the exciting uses of the new technologies, the challenge of e-connectivity is in determining the best way to manage it—and who should manage it. Governmental organizations should ask the following questions regarding policies and procedures:

- What is the jurisdiction's policy on social networking sites and applications?

- Who determines which websites and applications may be used? What criteria are used to make this determination?

- What safeguards, including policy, enforcement, and hardware, are in place to ensure the highest level of network infrastructure security from all possible malicious threats and intrusions?

- What processes and procedures are in place to monitor sites to which the public may contribute?

- What processes and procedures are in place to thwart the spread of false or harmful information? In other words, how will the organization respond to misinformation—which in a worst-case scenario could lead to a panic or other crisis?

- Moving forward, what will be the role of public-access cable channels? How can public-access television measure up when so many citizens are using web-based technologies?

- Who is in charge? Are today's web managers equipped with the necessary people skills, training, and management skills to coordinate multiple web-based communication platforms?

- How does e-connectivity fit in with a local, state, or federal agency's mission?

- Who will be the senior person to coordinate all online communications?

- How will success or failure be measured? Each organization should have a set of metrics that can be used to periodically assess the performance of, and satisfaction with, online programs and services.

- How do the organization's new social media policies affect records retention requirements and other existing policies and procedures?

Our world continues to become more web-centric as new kinds of online technologies are developed. It is very exciting to watch this growth, but governments at all levels desperately need to do more than just casually observe the changes. Citizens will expect nothing less.

Discussion Questions

1. What are the consequences for public managers who ignore the web-centric trend of the pocket computer/phone? What are the opportunities?

2. What are the consequences for public managers who ignore technology's potential in the areas of transparency and citizen engagement? What are the opportunities?

3. How can public sector organizations respond to the social networking phenomenon? What are the risks of ignoring it?

4. What are the pitfalls and opportunities associated with a virtual and/ or viral environment?

5. What are the implications for government of improved video and related e-connectivity technologies?

CHAPTER 14

Web 2.0's Knowledge Management Potential in the Public Sector

Tracy Haugen

To begin addressing how to manage knowledge, one must first think about where the knowledge resides. In the public sector, the work environment is changing, and much knowledge resides in the multi-sector workforce, which comprises three main elements:

- Political government appointees, who are largely in charge of setting policy for the agency

- Career government employees, who execute the administration of policies and programs

- Contractors, who are hired to provide services under the direction of government employees (either appointee or career).

Clearly, many other supporting players are involved in program execution—other agencies and jurisdictions (state, local, or foreign governments), the academic community and nonprofits—and these elements further complicate the modern government work environment.

If one also considers the dynamic nature of the governmental workforce, due to military and foreign service rotations, limited-term political appointments, and a more transient career workforce that, no longer satiated by hefty pensions, changes positions more frequently, then getting a handle on the knowledge management challenge seems even more daunting. In fact, government entities can have an easier time leveraging knowledge from their contractors than from their own workforce simply by stipulating the specifications or requirements in the procurement process. Thus, knowledge managers must consider the different segments and sources of work products when designing a knowledge management strategy.

Moreover, because the nature of governmental work is increasingly knowledge-based and requires less transaction processing, much of the knowledge resides in the workers' heads as they solve problems in real time. Therefore, a knowledge management strategy should seek to capture this tacit (or unshared) knowledge and expand its scope to accommodate the multi-sector workforce.

Capturing Tacit Knowledge through Web 2.0

If we accept that government seeks to benefit from its tacit knowledge, then employing Web 2.0 applications should be a key part of the strategy for capturing and managing this knowledge. Web 2.0 comprises a variety of online tools intended to facilitate knowledge sharing and collaboration (see Table 12-1). Web 2.0 captures knowledge as part of task execution in the *primary* work function, not as separable collateral duties which often become highly segmented. Asking work group members to contribute to a *wiki*, a website that allows visitors to edit and collaborate, contextualizes the knowledge captured and has a direct impact on meeting the work objective.

Web 2.0's open environment and use of informal networks allows an organization to transcend traditional bureaucratic knowledge management structures, another key challenge to be overcome in today's government work setting.

Web 2.0 has transformational potential. The ability to work more seamlessly, without geographic constraints, and even asynchronously, without time constraints, widens the possibilities for collaboration within and across agencies.

Table 14-1: Web 2.0 Tools

Web 2.0 tool	Business objective	Selected example
Blog ("Web"+"log") • Informal journal addressing any topic • Allows users to post news and commentary and embed multimedia components • Encompasses a broad range of content and formats • Integrates tools to pull content • Easy to embed in existing websites/content.	• Information sharing • Myth busting	• TSA's blog (U.S. Transportation Security Administration) • Communities @ State (U.S. Department of State)
Wiki: "All of us are smarter than any one of us." • Open content encyclopedias that allow users to comment on, share, and collaboratively distribute information • The user community is responsible for content maintenance.	• Best practices • Co-collaboration • Idea generation/innovation market • Process improvement	• Intellipedia (Office of the Director of National Intelligence) • Diplopedia (U.S. Department of State) • TSA's Idea Factory
Social networking applications/jams • Build virtual communities • Create "presence" where an audience already gathers • Allow users to communicate while also allowing people to link based on communities of interest • Provide insight into how information and influence flow.	• Expertise management/locator • Networking • Building trust across silos	• GovLoop • Politicopia (State of Utah) • Twitter

So how can these new tools help address the challenges of strategic knowledge management? As discussed earlier, Web 2.0 captures the tacit knowledge through primary work activities. Web 2.0 is a solution to the problem of tacit knowledge capture. It lays the foundation for knowledge management by allowing users to locate and share expertise and analyze the information needed to make better decisions.

Tacit Knowledge

Often, employees are given policy guidelines or standard operating procedures that they are supposed to use to determine how best to address a situation. Online forums allow users to tap into networks of fellow practitioners for advice on how to address nuanced business problems that aren't easily addressed with such formal procedures. Discussion blogs, wikis, and other collaboration tools can help a user capture ideas from the multisector workforce in real time to address live situations. This knowledge sharing may happen in the hallway or on the phone, but if it happens through an online forum, such an exchange of information can be reviewed by subject matter experts for validation, shared among peers, and adapted to address similar questions.

For example, Communities @ State is an initiative launched by the U.S. Department of State to connect employees from across the agency to discuss issues or events, request or respond to requests for assistance, share knowledge, develop best practice solutions, and connect a network of interested and knowledgeable people. State's workforce is highly mobile and highly dispersed. With employees assigned to more than two dozen strategic business units domestically (primarily bureaus that cover specific regions or foreign policy subjects) and more than 260 embassies and offices abroad, a solution was needed to bridge gaps in communication and information sharing. Employees needed an easy and reliable knowledge management, collaboration, and information-sharing method that could be accessed throughout the world.

As of May 19, 2009, the program had 55 active communities. The communities fall into at least one of three categories: office- or bureau-based, topic-area-based, or professional-dialogue-based. PD in Europe, a bureau- and professional-dialogue-based community, allows public diplomacy staff from more than 40 European posts to share their public diplomacy best practices. Another highly successful bureau-based intermission community focuses on specific topics rather than a specific profession. The North American Partnership, a community of staff in the large U.S. diplomatic missions in Canada and Mexico, provides a forum to discuss common homeland security, commercial, economic, and environmental issues. Another community in the program spans all three categories. Iran Watchers allows staff in the Near East Affairs bureau to report and discuss Iran-related issues at the classified level.[1]

Decision Forensics

Emerging tools like DeepDebate (http://deepdebate.org) capture discussion threads or arguments about a question or issue in an atypical way: Comments are grouped by theme rather than chronologically, as they are on most open blogs. This allows all points and counterpoints to be captured and connected.

Why is a structure like this useful? One reason is that certain ideas or suggestions may not have been feasible at a particular point in time, but the underlying issues can change, making them more practicable. If the debate on these issues is laid out in a way that is easy to follow, the larger organization will be better able to understand how decisions were made and the points of view that were considered, creating greater transparency among stakeholders. This transparency will support the trust building needed for organizations with fewer boundaries, which we'll discuss in more detail later.

After-action reviews are greatly enhanced if the information that led to the decision is still available. It is easy to second-guess decisions in hindsight, but imagine the ability to review a decision by highlighting information known at the time to determine the efficacy of the decision-making process. Such rigorous reflection can be a fantastic leadership development component, including insights into what information is truly needed when faced with certain challenges or decisions.

Expertise Locators

As mentioned previously, the workforce is changing more frequently than in previous eras. We often hear that employees are unsure of who to talk to when they are faced with a large, complex problem. Social networking tools can help locate expertise within and across organizations. Position descriptions are usually written with compliance with human resources policy in mind, and they may not fully describe individuals' knowledge and expertise that could be applied to specific problems.

In June 2008, Young Government Leaders co-founder Steve Ressler launched GovLoop, a new social networking site that strives to build a strong online community connecting government professionals and promoting knowledge sharing. In an interview with Harvard public management professor Steve Kelman, Ressler explained,

> I wanted an informal place where people could connect, share their ideas, and ask other questions. Additionally, instead of only discussing with specific government groups, I wanted to engage a broader community—across agencies, associations, disciplines, grade levels and ages. I wanted to engage those people who might not be in the (Washington) D.C. area, might not be able to attend events after work, or simply feel more comfortable online. I wanted to engage those students interested in working in the public sector to share in conversations with others already there.

Ressler is also seeing early personal success stories immerge from Gov-Loop. For instance, he notes that "I already have a master's student in public administration at Iowa State who has connected with several government employees who have provided him advice and potential resources for his thesis." This "Facebook for Feds" includes individual social profiles, an events calendar, career resources, and a diverse collection of blogs.[2]

By viewing each employee as a whole person and as part of the voluntary workplace community, not only can we appreciate his or her strengths, but we are more likely to make connections at a personal level—a dimension critical for community trust-building.

Considerations for Implementing a Web 2.0 Strategy

Much has been written about the benefits of Web 2.0, some of which is more hype than thoughtful analysis. Those who might have assumed that

Web 2.0 would be a passing fad are probably more bullish on its staying power after seeing its significant impact on the recent presidential election and the White House's subsequent emphasis on Web 2.0 technologies. However, Web 2.0 is not a panacea that can be used blindly to solve every problem. The tools can be used to extend current knowledge management and communications toolsets, but using them this way may not tap into the full power a Web 2.0 strategy and culture can bring. I will discuss some of the unique considerations for implementing Web 2.0.

Resetting Expectations about Knowledge Management

The notion of managing knowledge implies that there is an underlying sense of hierarchy and control in historical management models. The Web 2.0 culture is based on an opt-in mentality. Moderating input to Web 2.0 tools is generally a grassroots effort. In fact, if the effort to manage knowledge and contributions smells too much like a mandate, typical early adopters may resist participating due to this external pressure alone. Part of the appeal of Web 2.0 technologies is the opportunity they create for users to rally to a common cause (e.g., interest in networking with other young professionals, collaborating on related research topics or management challenges).

What does this mean for management in a practical sense? Interested parties must be given the freedom to co-create the knowledge-capture program and, if necessary, take it in different directions than originally imagined. The success of the effort depends in part on how it was launched. The sponsor of a Web 2.0 tool must be open, authentic, and real. If it is perceived to be too "headquarters" or party line, then it may not capture the hearts and minds of its users.

Management's role may shift from managing knowledge to inspiring knowledge-capture and drumming up energy and interest in the tool. This energy is essential: There are plenty of dormant wikis and blogs that did not attract attention or garner participation, in part because the inspirational element was missing.

A U.S. Transportation Security Administration (TSA) employee website, IdeaFactory, is an example of a tool that has inspired agency workers to collaborate on the issues they deem important—without mandating the issues to focus on. In April 2007, TSA launched the IdeaFactory, a forum on which employees can post their suggestions for improving agency operations. As of July 2009, there were 4,500 suggestions on IdeaFactory, and employees have added more than 58,000 posts to vote for specific suggestions. The number of general comments posted now exceeds 39,000.[3] Only the ideas that generate the highest ratings and votes are promoted to the next round of consideration for possible implementation. The site allows the community to weigh in on the feasibility of the ideas and agree on top priorities, thus generating broader community buy-in and making implementation easier due to a shared sense of idea ownership.

Allowing for a Learning Curve

Web 2.0 is meant to operate in a flatter, more open environment. Many government institutions have not traditionally operated in this manner and may not be aware of the unintended consequences. Governments experimenting with blogs may not initially be aware that that up to 15 percent of blog comments will be negative. Negative comments are not necessarily bad; they imply that the blog is credible and not overly controlled by the host. But imagine the initial reaction of an unsuspecting deputy secretary when negative comments are posted and the team is not prepared to handle the situation.

Taking proactive action—for example, posting rules of engagement and a firm statement that abusive comments will be removed—can help mitigate some of these risks. In addition, government blog administrators can encourage blog readers to report unwarranted negative comments or counter them with relevant facts. Such a system might be more effective than simply censoring or closing off discussion. The process of reading, responding to, and approving comments on Web 2.0 sites often evolves naturally over time, as the leadership better understands the community and issues it wants to address.

The TSA's blog (http://www.tsa.gov/blog) was launched at the urging of the agency's former administrator, Kip Hawley. Hawley pushed to make the blog happen because he believed that an open and transparent blog was a powerful forum for communicating directly with TSA's customer base. A TSA blogger explained, "When Kip started the TSA blog, honesty is what he was after. He wanted it, warts and all. We sometimes get pushback from our officers in the field though. At times, it can seem as if we've tied ourselves to the whipping post and created a demoralization machine. But that's not true at all."[4]

Hawley and other forward-looking leaders realize the power of public comments; now they can be discounted by peers. An organization will need sufficient time and experience to get used to administering a public blog, so pilot efforts are highly recommended.

Clarifying Decision-Making Authority

For collaborative sites such as blogs and wikis, be clear in your user instructions about what the community is being asked to provide. Are members part of an open community, or are they being asked to contribute different inputs and opinions that reflect their particular expertise? While much has been made of the wisdom of crowds, it is unlikely that top agency policy will be decided by someone who simply logs into a wiki. However, there is great benefit in getting diverse perspectives that allow policymakers to consider many different ideas before they make a decision. For example, the State of Utah launched a site called Politicopia (www.politicopia.com) to collect input from citizens on bills coming up for a vote. A bill on school vouchers drew many comments that several legislators sited as influencing their stand on the bill.[5]

Ensuring Adequate Stakeholder Representation

There is an adoption curve for Web 2.0. While its tools are not used solely by one generation, there is a "digital native" demographic that is very comfortable with the use of wikis, blogs, and texting, while the older generation may be less familiar with these same tools. One must be wary of unintended biases when collecting input through Web 2.0 channels. There is still a digital divide; for example, less-affluent communities are less likely to have Internet access. These inequalities can be overcome, but they definitely need to be considered when seeking to collect a wide range of input from a large spectrum of stakeholders.

Determining How to Accredit Expertise

The Wikipedia entry on the "free encyclopedia's" own history documents the difficulty of trying to determine who should have the authority to provide "expertise." Each of Wikipedia's founders espoused a different school of thought:

> [Creator Jimmy] Wales, a believer in communal governance and "hands off" executive management, went on to establish self-governance and bottom-up self-direction by editors on Wikipedia. He made it clear that he would not be involved in the community's day to day management, but would encourage it to learn to self-manage and find its own best approaches. As of 2007, Wales mostly restricts his own role to occasional input on serious matters, executive activity, advocacy of knowledge, and encouragement of similar reference projects.
>
> [Co-creator Larry] Sanger advocated a "two tier" expert-led culture and more 'hands on' executive management, with final editorial control by chief editors closer to the traditional model. He returned briefly to academia, then after joining the Digital Universe Foundation, went on to found Citizendium, an alternative open encyclopedia which uses real names for contributors in order to reduce disruptive editing, supports the specific recognition of experts, and is governed by a system of top-down management, including himself or agreed-upon editors or committees. He has stated that he intends to leave in a few years, when the project and its management are established.[6]

Depending on the business need, a hands-off approach might be appropriate; the community itself decides which assertions are valid and should be promoted. However, if the topic is very sophisticated or the timing urgent, a more controlled expertise model may be warranted.

Unifying under a Common Cause

Participation across diverse groups is greatly facilitated if the groups recognize a common cause that can unite them. Knowledge sharing or collaboration requires an underlying level of trust and an ability to relate to other members of the community. Many civil servants are sufficiently motivated by the agency mission to transcend organizational conflicts. Allow venues for the groups to authenticate their commitment to the common cause (e.g., through blogs, podcasts, e-forums, etc.) and the contributions each brings will help generate energy and drive for knowledge-sharing and collaboration. Stephen Covey has written a book, *The Speed of Trust*, illustrating how trust has a direct impact on the speed and cost of work. The greater the trust, the faster work can be done and the lower the costs. If there is low trust, then every action has to be mandated and enforced, thus slowing the process and further decreasing trust. Covey explains:

> Take communications. In a high-trust relationship, you can say the wrong things and people will still get your meaning. In a low-trust relationship, you can be very measured, even precise, and they'll still misinterpret you.[7]

Conclusion

The last consideration discussed in this chapter, trust building, is the most important of all. When trust is established and motivations are clear, forgiveness for any bumps along the way is more likely to be shown. As the use of Web 2.0 functions grows, promoted by the current administration, we stand at the beginning of what will surely be an interesting era in knowledge management.

Discussion Questions

1. What is tacit knowledge and how can government capture it through Web 2.0?

2. How does the U.S. Department of State employ tacit knowledge to connect employees from across the agency and connect a worldwide network of interested and knowledgeable people?

3. What is decision forensics and how can this tool create greater transparency across stakeholders?

4. What managerial expectations may need to be reset as we move into the brave new world of Web 2.0, particularly regarding the underlying sense of hierarchy and control in historical management models?

5. What are the keys to success in building trust as part of a dynamic Web 2.0 agency rollout?

Notes

1. National Academy of Pubic Administration, "Communities at State," (case study from Collaboration Project), http://www.collaborationproject.org/display/case/Communities+at+State (accessed September 18, 2009).
2. Steve Kelman, "The Lectern: GovLoop Gives the Public Sector Community a Voice," *Federal Computer Weekly* (July 11, 2009), http://fcw.com/blogs/lectern/2008/07/the-lectern-govloop-gives-the-public-sector-community-a-voice.aspx (accessed September 18, 2009).
3. Brian Bain, "4 Studies in Collaboration; Case 2: TSA's IdeaFactory," *Federal Computer Weekly* (February 29, 2008), http://fcw.com/articles/2008/02/29/4-studies-in-collaboration-151-case-2-tsa146s-ideafactory.aspx (accessed September 18, 2009).
4. Steve Radick, "An Interview with Blogger Bob from TSA's Evolution of Security Blog," *Social Media Strategery* (March 10, 2009), http://steveradick.com/2009/03/10/an-interview-with-blogger-bob-from-tsas-evolution-of-security-blog/ (accessed September 18, 2009).
5. National Academy of Public Administration, "Utah Politicopia," Collaboration Project website, http://www.collaborationproject.org/display/case/Utah+Politicopia (accessed September 18, 2009).
6. Wikipedia, "History of Wikipedia," http://en.wikipedia.org/wiki/Wikipedia_History (accessed September 18, 2009).
7. Stephen M.R. Covey, *The Speed of Trust* (New York: Free Press, 2006), 6.

PART 5

Strategic Acquisition Management

Contracting for Services in State and Local Government

Robert Shick

In only eight years (fiscal years 2000 to 2008), federal government spending on contracts has grown 152.7 percent, from $208.3 billion to $526.5 billion. While comparable data are not available for the 89,527 state and local governments in the United States, almost all aspects of state and local government, from waste management to correctional facilities, are touched in some way by contracting. The consistent argument for contracting out work is that doing business in the competitive marketplace reduces costs and improves quality.

Concurrently, the body of academic literature on contracting has grown. Such authors as Steven Cohen and William Eimicke; Phillip Cooper; John Donahue; Elliott Sclar; E. S. Savas; William Curry; Steven Smith and Michael Lipsky; Stephen Goldsmith; Carol Ascher, Norm Fruchter, and Robert Berne; Charles Brecher and Sheila Spiezo; and the American Federation of State, County and Municipal Employees and AFL-CIO have all published on the topic. Some of these authors believe contracting should play an increasingly important role in the delivery of government services, while others are more cautious about its use and resultant benefits.

There is also concern that contracting out government services blurs the public perception of the role of government: Is the government or the contractor responsible for these services? While the government is ultimately responsible for contracted services, the public's uncertainty diffuses and confuses the role of government in society.

Elements of Government Contracting

This chapter addresses the state of the field of contracting for state and local government services, the most important recent research about contracting, and lessons for the future. To begin, government contracting should be considered a holistic process that comprises a number of elements, each important in its own right. The elements of government contracting are:

- The make or buy decision

- The contract document

- The solicitation and selection of contractors

- Contract administration, including the relationship with the contractor

- Evaluation of the contractor's performance

- Using contractor performance information to make future contracting decisions.

Government contracting works best and achieves its goals—reduced costs and improved quality—when each of these elements is managed effectively. This means that a government should not focus on one or a couple of the elements at the expense of other elements. All too often, government concentrates on the solicitation and selection of contractors and devotes far too little attention to evaluating the performance of contractors. This is comparable to determining where to buy something and at what price but not paying attention to whether you are satisfied with the purchase. In the public sector, inattention to evaluating contractors' performance implies that a government is unconcerned about whether it cuts costs, increases quality, and is accountable to its citizens.

The Make or Buy Decision

The make or buy decision, the initial step in government contracting, has often been approached from the perspective of political philosophy rather than careful analysis. This decision becomes an extension of the argument that smaller government is better government, and services can be delivered more efficiently and effectively by external for-profit or nonprofit organizations. This may be true for some government functions, but not for others. The determining factor in this decision should be analysis, not philosophy.

Another important question is whether the service being considered for contracting is a core competency of government. Invariably, core competencies are not meant to be contracted out, while the disposition of non-core functions is a business decision. Government is responsible for administering complex institutions, such as hospitals. The core function in hospitals is health care, not laundry services. In school systems, the core function is education, not the transportation of students.

The cost analysis to determine whether to contract should include as many of the costs and benefits as can be calculated. This analysis compares the potential new delivery system to the existing one. For the current system, the cost analysis takes into account the cost of staff salaries, fringe benefits, equipment, and overhead. For the new delivery system, this analysis includes the estimated costs charged by the contractor and government staff, as well as fringe benefits that will be required to manage the contract (a cost that is often overlooked, as are the skills that are required to manage a contract).

It is understood that for an initial analysis, the costs of contracting are estimated. However, information on contractor costs from other government entities should be used to create this estimate. A cost analysis provides the government with a realistic estimate of projected savings (if there are to be any) and the ability to decide whether to make or buy products or services from a cost perspective.

The Contract Document

The contract document presents the responsibilities of the government and those of the contractor. During preparation of the contract document, the focus is generally on ensuring that the requirements of the contract are stated in sufficient detail. For example, in a contract for foster care services, is it sufficient to state a field visit should be made with certain objectives, or should it also specify a minimum length of time for the visit?

The contract is also the record of government and contractor accountability—specifically, the metrics or indicators the contractor is required to achieve. The contract document indicates whether the contractor is obligated to achieve minimum performance levels for payment (i.e., a performance contract). The performance metrics can be based on input, output, outcome, or process measures. Without these benchmarks in the contract, government can hold the contractor accountable for only more general objectives, such as providing a "quality service," but with no definition of how to measure quality.

While outcome measures have become the gold standard in the field of performance measurement, for some service areas, such as health care, education, and child care, which are very complex, it has been difficult to develop accepted outcome measures. Because of this, a combination of input, output, outcome, and process measures are used to assess performance and accountability. This is evidenced in home health care contracting: Government examines the credentials of the providers (input), the number of nursing visits made (output), the overall well-being of clients (outcome), and the time frames for the completion of tasks (process).

A contract, therefore, is not just the concern of government lawyers. It is the accountability document and the purview of program service specialists as well (e.g., contract officers, contracting officer technical representatives, etc.).

Solicitation and Selection of Contractors

Requests for proposals (RFPs) have allowed considerable progress in the solicitation of service contractors because they have standardized the solicitation process. There is a set format for the contents of an RFP, which establishes procedures the government and potential contractors will follow (for example, whether pre-bidding conferences will be held), how proposals should be submitted, and the confidentiality of the information submitted.

The first step in the evaluation process is determining whether each proposal is responsive to the solicitation and whether the proposer can be considered a responsible bidder (i.e., it is capable of performing the requirements of the contract). Evaluation of proposals should begin with establishing criteria and, often, determining the weights of each component of the proposal (such as the qualifications of the staff, the prospective contractor's experience with similar contracts, the budget, and the program plan). The weights given to each part of a proposal are very important and can influence which contractor is selected. For example, placing more emphasis on experience with similar contracts will favor entities that fit this criterion and hinder those with less experience, even if they propose excellent budgets and program plans.

Individuals or teams can perform the proposal evaluations. Each team member may have different areas of expertise (e.g., financial, program). More than one team may evaluate each proposal to achieve balance in the process. These evaluations often yield numerical scores, which facilitate comparison of the proposals. One or more contractors can be chosen at this point if the goal is to select those with the highest scores that meet the service needs of the government. Alternatively, the government may choose, for example, the six highest-scoring proposers by setting a cut-off score, then taking further steps to select the winning contractor—interviewing the proposers, performing site visits at the proposers' offices, and/or negotiating the cost and operation of the contract with each proposer.

All of the steps in the solicitation and selection processes are important and should be considered carefully by the government in order to recruit the organizations that will best be able to fulfill the terms of the contract.

Contract Administration and the Government's Relationship with the Contractor

Contract administration requires more attention from governments. Too often, government does not provide the appropriate resources for this function. Governments seem to assume that once a contract is set, the contractor will fulfill its responsibilities. Also, when resources *are* provided for contract administration, the skills needed to perform this important responsibility are not adequately recognized.

Contract administration and the government's relationship with the contractor are essential functions that help ensure that services are delivered according to the specifications in the contract document. Government should devote the resources needed to fund qualified staff in sufficient numbers for these functions.

A variety of skills are necessary to manage contract relationships under service contracts, including interpersonal skills, knowledge of the contract document and its requirements, knowledge of the service being delivered, organizational management, and financial management. While the contract administrator may not have all of these skills, he or she should have access to staff competent in these areas.

Effectively managed contract administration and relationships with contractors are especially critical for service contracts, under which there is usually ongoing communication between the government and the contractor regarding the clients receiving the government-funded services. Homeless shelters, foster care, and home health care are examples of government-run services that are often performed by contractors. In many cases, the government evaluates client service needs, then refers clients to contracted service providers. The government then communicates with the service contractor about each client's status and needs.

Evaluation of Contractor Performance

Although evaluating contractor performance is part of contract administration, we highlight it here to emphasize its significance. Evaluating a contractor's performance is the government's primary method of keeping contractors accountable. Like contract administration, evaluation has not been given adequate attention and resources by government.

The government should state in the contract document the performance measures it will use. Different performance measures provide different degrees of confidence in the results. Some governments ask contractors to periodically self-report their performance data. This method requires fewer government resources because the contractor provides all of the performance information, but it necessitates that the government trust the contractor to provide accurate information.

Other government organizations visit the contractor on-site, interview contractor staff, and complete a random sample of records to measure performance. This is a more reliable performance measurement approach, as the contractor does not know which records will be examined or the government staff that will gather the information.

Still others combine the above methods. This is probably the most comprehensive and effective method for gathering performance information. In general, some metrics can be self-reported, such as input and output measures, while others need additional attention, such as outcome and process measures. Additionally, the mixed-method approach combining self-reporting and site visits enables the government to verify information the contractor has provided.

Using Contractor Performance Information to Make Decisions

Performance information is useful—if it influences government decisions. These decisions are principally of two types: managing poor-performing contractors and making future determinations about contracting. Many governments deal with poor-performing contractors by providing technical assistance that helps them—for example, modifying internal operating systems and record keeping systems. The government then monitors the contractor's performance to determine if there has been improvement.

A contractor's past performance should be one of the primary considerations when a government makes future contracting decisions, though other factors (such as competition from other vendors) may influence whether a contractor is retained for a new term. The re-contracting determination is one of the most important reasons for holding government accountable for its policies. Poor-performing contractors that have been given an opportunity, but have failed, to improve their performance undermine the reasons for outsourcing a government function—reduced costs and increased quality. When government does not react appropriately to negative performance information, it is not demonstrating accountability to its citizens in the use of tax dollars.

Conclusion

Contracting for services by state and local governments has become an increasingly important government function. This trend will probably continue, based on the conviction that contracting, through the market and competition, will allow government to reduce the costs and increase the quality of the services it provides.

The question at this juncture is: How can government perform the contracting function to ensure the best outcome for its citizens? The six elements of contracting described in this chapter represent a holistic approach to contracting that requires sufficient attention and resources from government. This is especially true for three elements: contract administration, measuring contractor performance, and using performance information to make future contracting decisions. Government will achieve its goals and be more accountable to citizens to the extent that it focuses on these essential elements.

Discussion Questions

1. What should be the pivotal drivers of the make-or-buy decision?

2. How can the contract document serve as an accountability tool for program service specialists?

3. What strategic management elements are involved in soliciting and selecting contractors?

4. What key elements are involved in evaluating contractor performance and using contractor performance information?

5. How can government perform the contracting function in a way that ensures the best outcome for citizens?

Recommended Resources

American Federation of State, County and Municipal Employees and AFL-CIO. "Passing the Bucks: The Contracting Out of Public Services." Washington, D.C., 1984.

Ascher, Carol, Norm Fruchter, and Robert Berne. *Hard Lessons: Public Schools and Privatization*. New York: Twentieth Century Fund, 1996.

Brecher, Charles, and Sheila Spiezo. *Privatization and Public Hospitals*. New York: Twentieth Century Fund, 1995.

Cohen, Steven, and William Eimicke. *The Responsible Contract Manager: Protecting the Public Interest in an Outsourced World*. Washington, D.C.: Georgetown University Press, 2008.

Cooper, Phillip. *Governing by Contract: Challenges and Opportunities for Public Managers*. Washington, D.C.: CQ Press, 2003.

Curry, William Sims. *Contracting for Services in State and Local Government Agencies*. Boca Raton, FL: CRC Press, 2009.

Donahue, John. *The Privatization Decision: Public Ends, Private Means*. New York: Basic Books, 1989.

Goldsmith, Stephen. *The Twenty-First Century City: Resurrecting Urban America*. Lanham, MD: Rowman & Litchfield Publishers, 1999.

Savas, E. S. *Privatization in the City: Successes, Failures, Lessons*. Washington, D.C.: CQ Press, 2005.

Savas, E. S. *Privatization and Public-Private Partnerships*. New York: Seven Bridges Press, 2000.

Sclar, Elliott. *You Don't Always Get What You Pay For: The Economics of Privatization*. Ithaca, NY: Cornell University Press, 2000.

Smith, Steven, and Michael Lipsky. *Nonprofits for Hire: The Welfare State in the Age of Contracting*. Cambridge, MA: Harvard University Press, 1993.

U.S. Census Bureau. "Federal, State, and Local Governments: 2007 Census of Governments." Washington, D.C., 2007. http://www.census.gov/govs/www/cog2007.html (accessed September 18, 2009).

USASpending.gov, http://www.usaspending.gov/.

PART 6

Strategic Performance
Management

CHAPTER 16

Citistat: Evaluating City Management in Baltimore, Maryland

James Horton

Performance measurement in local government continues to be an elusive target at the dawn of the 21st century. Issues of efficiency, effectiveness, accountability, and transparency continue to be problematic for public administrators. They must work with limited resources and engage citizens, and they are expected to emulate the private sector. Governments at all levels have implemented a variety of performance measurement programs since Clarence Ridley wrote in 1938, "It is not enough to be honest, but governments must be efficient as well." Today, as public administrators continue their quest toward improving local government, "stat" performance measurement systems are sweeping the nation. Known originally as Compstat, this unique performance measurement method combines specific management techniques with technology in an effort to improve local government performance.

Compstat

Compstat originated with the New York City Police Department (NYPD) in 1994 under the leadership of police commissioner William J. Bratton. Compstat was not a pre-packaged system adapted from the private sector, but rather the culmination of Bratton's efforts to reduce crime, enhance agency performance, and improve data collection. The name Compstat comes from the computer file name given to the first set of comparative crime statistics used to evaluate the New York City crime problem.[1]

According to Moore,[2] Compstat is a strategic management system combined with administrative and technical innovations. Compstat is further described as a new paradigm in police management and one of the most important innovations in policing for the last decade.[3] In 1996, Compstat was awarded the Innovations in American Government Award from Harvard University's Kennedy School of Government.

Citistat

While meeting with Jack Maple of the NYPD about Compstat, Baltimore mayor Martin O'Malley realized that the system could be used to manage an entire city.[4] Following his election in 2000, O'Malley began using a system dubbed Citistat to manage a few departments. According to Behn,[5] "Citistat is Compstat applied to an entire city." Today, current Baltimore mayor Sheila Dixon continues to use Citistat to manage Baltimore, and government officials from across the country frequently visit to learn more about it.

During its first year of operation, Citistat is credited with saving the city $13.2 million and by 2007 had accumulated $350 million in total savings.[6] In addition, Baltimore was also able to reduce absenteeism and overtime. By combining Citistat with a centralized 311 nonemergency request line, Baltimore was also able to serve its citizens better. In 2004, Citistat was recognized with the Innovations in American Government Award from Harvard University's Kennedy School of Government. This chapter discusses Citistat's historical origins, structural composition, and theoretical orientation.

Historical Origins

Upon his election, Mayor Martin O'Malley inherited a city with many problems. Baltimore suffered from fiscal distress, high crime rates, and disenfranchised employees.[7] Citistat allowed O'Malley to stay in frequent contact with department directors and prioritize the work of each department. To accomplish this, O'Malley first established performance targets for each department and next began to implement a service culture that put the citizen first.[8]

The NYPD tried to improve quality of life by focusing on minor problems—"broken windows"—but O'Malley took a much more direct approach. He established a 311 non-emergency request line, which helped him learn exactly what the citizens wanted, and he focused city departments directly on those needs. O'Malley became famous for his guarantee that requests to fill potholes would be accomplished within 48 hours.

Mission clarification, or in Baltimore's case, establishing specific target objectives, is a key goal for agencies using Compstat. Furthermore, department directors are required to have an intimate knowledge of departmental workings and some plan for achieving these required target objectives.

To O'Malley, accomplishing specific targets with a focus on a service culture were compatible goals that could be accomplished through Citistat.[9] However, there is much more to Citistat than setting a performance target and waiting for citizens to phone in requests. Although each city using Citistat customizes it, it has specific structural components that will increase the probability of its success.

Structural Composition

Citistat cities are identifiable because, using data, they conduct frequent meetings to discuss past performance, future objectives, and performance strategies to accomplish those objectives.[10] This definition may categorize Citistat cities, but it does not identify or explain the necessary underlying structural components needed to make Citistat a successful performance management strategy. In an earlier article,[11] Behn identified six core drivers of Citistat:

- The active engagement of the city's top executives

- The timeliness and scope of the data as well as its analysis

- The perseverance of the questioning, feedback, and follow-up

- The consequences for good, poor, and improved performance

- A focus on problem-solving, continuous experimentation, and learning

- The institutional memory of the city's top executives.

Together, these components provide a blueprint for city leaders to follow. They are reinforced at the frequent meetings synonymous with Citistat. Behn[12] admits that even he is not sure which of the drivers are most important, but he believes that collectively they have great power.

Active Engagement of Top Executives

The active engagement of the city's top executives has two components. First, Behn[13] suggests that city leaders must be committed and show this commitment by investing their personal time. Without a positive commitment to success, department directors may dismiss Citistat as a recent fad that is sure to be short-lived. Second, city leaders must set a direction. In Baltimore, O'Malley set specific performance targets. For Compstat, it was the clear mission to reduce crime. For Citistat to be successful, department directors must have a direction to follow and a specific goal to achieve. By establishing specific performance targets, O'Malley gave department directors personal responsibility for achieving them.[14]

Timeliness and Scope of Data

The timeliness and scope of data collected are essential to the operation of any organization; cities are no different. The data must be both timely and relevant.[15] In Baltimore, a Citistat analyst from the mayor's office thoroughly reviews the data, and Citistat meetings are frequent and consistent. Department directors make presentations to the mayor on a set biweekly schedule and often conduct their own "agency stat"[16] by meeting before presenting in an effort to identify areas of concern. Data for Citistat discussions can be drawn from any number of sources, including departmental records, 311 service requests, or an independent Citistat investigator assigned to the mayor's office. The most important function of the data is to spark discussion about a department's performance and help decisionmakers choose managerial strategies.[17]

Perseverance of Questioning, Feedback, and Follow-Up

In Baltimore, unlike at most city departmental performance meetings, the department director does not control the agenda—the mayor does.[18] And the agenda, which consists of questioning, feedback, and follow-up, is dependent on the data and performance of a department. Citistat was specifically designed *not* to be just a presentation of data. Instead, it is a two-way discussion of data and performance.[19] This discussion takes place between city leaders and department directors. Important to the success of Citistat is the expectation that questions be specific, the feedback intelligently informed, and unanswered issues positively resolved. The meetings must have a purpose and must be beneficial.[20]

Consequences for Good, Poor, and Improved Performance

The consequences for good, poor, and improved performance underscore the emphasis on accountability. In Baltimore, Citistat identified poorly performing department directors, who were eventually replaced. However, the fear of job loss is not the only motivating factor. More important, there is always another Citistat presentation due within two weeks. The need to answer questions regarding department performance is a consequence in itself.[21] That the meetings are attended by peers, superiors, and subordinates adds stress to the situation.

Focus on Problem Solving, Continuous Experimentation, and Learning

Citistat provides an ideal forum for organizational learning because it frequently brings together city leaders and department directors for the sole purpose of discussing organizational performance. At Citistat meetings, there should be a focus on problem-solving, continuous experimentation, and learning. According to Behn,[22] city leaders and department directors are all responsible for improving performance. Citistat facilitates two-way discussion. Behn[23] describes the meeting process as "less hierarchal, more collegial than the conspicuous layout of the room or the obvious direction of the questioning might suggest."

Institutional Memory of Top Executives

Finally, institutional memory reinforces the previous five core components. Without frequent meetings between city leaders and department directors, it becomes difficult to recognize when a department has actually improved its performance.[24] These meetings not only reinforce expectations and ensure accountability, but also build trust. This trust can further motivate individuals and the organization to accomplish more.

Theoretical Orientation

While the structural components of Citistat provide a framework for cities to follow, they do not identify the system's underlying values. It is important for city leaders to understand these values as they embark on implementing Citistat. The system does present a challenge to contemporary public management thinking in its emphasis on and expression of the values of accountability, *efficiency*, and transparency. Similar to Compstat, Citistat promotes accountability and transparency, but it subtly replaces Compstat's focus on *effectiveness* with efficiency.

Accountability

Accountability for Citistat is assigned to department directors, who report to the mayor on a biweekly basis in a public forum to discuss the performance of their departments. The questioning of these directors sets the tone and helps to establish personal responsibility.[25] According to Behn,[26] "Citistat is a confrontational, accountability-holding process." One of Baltimore's unique features is the strength of the mayoral position. Through Citistat, the strong mayor is afforded a powerful system to exercise control over the bureaucracy and implement his or her agenda.[27]

Transparency

Transparency is another feature replicated from Compstat. Baltimore's Citistat meetings are conducted in a public forum with peers, superiors, and subordinates present. The meetings typically involve the city's management team, though guests from other city government elements are often present. In addition, reports submitted by departments for the purpose of review and evaluation are posted on a public website maintained by the city. The transparency of Citistat motivates department directors to achieve performance targets.[28]

Efficiency

Efficiency was implicitly expressed in O'Malley's performance targets. It is evident that O'Malley believed the Baltimore bureaucracy was unresponsive and underperforming.[29] Therefore, he established performance targets in Baltimore with the intention of accomplishing more outputs.[30] Service requests were O'Malley's bottom line.[31] This stands in contrast to Bratton's efforts with the NYPD to focus more on a particular outcome, reducing crime. For O'Malley and the citizens of Baltimore, outputs *were* the outcomes. According to Behn,[32] "A city government delivers concrete services. Thus, citizens perceive improved outputs to be improved outcomes." O'Malley's outcome was citizen satisfaction with a responsive and productive city. He was concerned more with results than with quality.[33]

Baltimore, beyond producing more outputs and responding to citizen nonemergency requests, should define desired socially desirable outcomes and decide which outputs will have the greatest impact on achieving them. Citizen satisfaction is surely one type of outcome, especially if you are interested in reelection. But it is not the only outcome.

Conclusion

Citistat is a unique system for managing an entire city government. Using this system, former Baltimore mayor Martin O'Malley did an exceptional job of gaining control of the city's bureaucracy and focusing city government on increasing productivity and accepting a service-oriented culture that put citizens first. It appears Citistat was successful because O'Malley established clear performance targets and provided leadership by committing his time to the effort.

In Baltimore, Citistat promoted three primary values: accountability, efficiency, and transparency. The true outcome was citizen satisfaction. There are currently no studies to determine if residents of Baltimore are better off after Citistat, but it appears that they are satisfied. O'Malley, now the elected governor of the state of Maryland, has since embarked on a journey to apply Citistat to state government.

Discussion Questions

1. What is Compstat and why is it considered an important tool for public administrators? Discuss how Compstat worked in New York City.

2. What is Citistat? Discuss how Citistat worked in Baltimore.

3. How does accountability fit into the Citistat process? Why is feedback an important element of Citistat?

4. Discuss the relationship of outputs to outcomes in the Citistat process.

5. How did Citistat promote the values of accountability, efficiency, and transparency in Baltimore?

6. Is there a downside to using Citistat?

Notes

1. Eli B. Silverman, *NYPD Battles Crime: Innovative Strategies in Policing* (Boston: Northeastern University Press, 1999).
2. Mark H. Moore, "Sizing Up Compstat: An Important Administrative Innovation in Policing," *Criminology and Public Policy* 2 (2003): 469.
3. Vincent E. Henry, *The Compstat Paradigm: Management Accountability in Policing, Business, and the Public Sector* (Flushing, NY: Looseleaf Law Publications, 2003); See note 1.
4. Robert D. Behn, "The Varieties of Citistat," *Public Administration Review* 66 (2006): 332; Teresita Perez and Reece Rushing, "The Citistat Model: How Data-Driven Government Can Increase Efficiency and Effectiveness," Center for American Progress (2007).

5. Robert D. Behn, "The Core Drivers of Citistat: It's Not Just About the Meetings and the Maps," *International Public Management Journal* 8 (2005): 295.

6. Teresita Perez and Reece Rushing, "The Citistat Model: How Data-Driven Government Can Increase Efficiency and Effectiveness," Center for American Progress (2007).

7. Ibid.

8. Robert D. Behn, "The Theory Behind Baltimore's Citistat," (paper presented at the 28th Annual Research Conference of the Association for Public Policy Analysis and Management, Madison, Wisconsin, 2006.

9. Ibid.

10. Robert D. Behn, "The Varieties of Citistat," *Public Administration Review* 66 (2006): 332.

11. See note 5.

12. Ibid.

13. Ibid.

14. See note 8.

15. See note 5.

16. Ibid.

17. See note 6; see note 8.

18. Robert D. Behn, "What All Mayors Would Like to Know about Baltimore's Citistat Performance Strategy," IBM Center for the Business of Government, 2007.

19. Lance deHaven-Smith and Kenneth C. Jenne, II, "Management by Inquiry: A Discursive Accountability System for Large Organizations," *Public Administration Review* 66 (2006): 64.

20. See note 10.

21. See note 5.

22. Ibid.

23. Ibid.

24. Ibid.

25. See note 19; see note 8.

26. See note 5.

27. See note 18.

28. Ibid.

29. See note 6; see note 18.

30. See note 18.

31. See note 5.

32. See note 8.

33. See note 18.

CHAPTER 17

Comparing Local Performance Management in the United Kingdom and United States

Peter McHugh

Mandatory. The reason performance management (PM) is so much more widespread in United Kingdom local government compared to United States city and county government boils down to this one word. The U.K. Audit Commission was established to ensure that U.K. local governments (called *councils*) deliver the highest standard of service for the best possible value. It monitors local governments' performance through the use of a mandatory set of national performance measures and a compulsory audit and inspection regime. The Audit Commission has this power because the U.K. central government provides the bulk of a council's funding, whereas U.S. local governments rely predominantly on property and sales taxes.

U.K. government performance evaluation began in 2000 with the introduction of best value performance indicators (BVPIs). There were hundreds of BVPIs, which measured performance across all service areas. Local governments had to report their performance on the BVPIs to central government every year. They also were required to produce an annual best value performance plan that compared their performance on the BVPIs to that of other local governments.

Best value evolved in 2002 into the Comprehensive Performance Assessment (CPA), which not only examined the performance of individual council services but also included a corporate assessment, part of which involved scoring the council's performance management skills on a 1 to 4 scale. Each council ended up with an overall CPA label: poor, weak, fair, good, or excellent.

As of April 2009, the CPA has been replaced with the Comprehensive Area Assessment (CAA), which shifts the emphasis away from individual councils toward partnerships that work between all public bodies involved in delivering local-priority outcomes. CAA comes with a new set of 198 national performance indicators that all U.K. councils must measure and report on.

Nurturing a Performance Culture

As a result of these continually evolving central government directives, U.K. councils have sharpened their performance management skills and in the process developed a range of relevant tools and approaches that nurture a performance culture. Here, we will look at six of these skill areas and contrast the situation with that at the local level in the United States:

- Creating a holistic performance management framework

- Aligning resources and activities with corporate goals

- Benchmarking against similar profile organizations

- Performance reporting to citizens

- Tracking performance in partnerships

- Using software to support the performance management process.

Creating a Holistic Performance Management Framework

Embedding a performance management culture requires staff engagement across the organization so that performance becomes an everyday priority. Critical to achieving this is a detailed framework specifying how performance will be managed in a practical sense and that links strategies, plans, policies, and indicators to enable monitoring of organizational performance. A good framework outlines the annual performance management cycle, synchronizing business planning and budgeting processes along with scheduling performance review forums or meetings.

A U.K. council performance management framework typically integrates three core elements—performance indicators, actions, and risks—into a holistic process with well-defined stages and a reporting/performance review cycle. A crucial element is communicating with staff and citizens by publishing performance data on the Internet. Over years, more and more examples have emerged of U.K. councils with high levels of staff engagement in performance management—from senior officers/managers and councillors/commissioners down to teams within departments—that are actively involved in managing operations in line with the council's strategic plan.

The use of formal performance management frameworks (such as Baldrige, ISO, and Sterling) in U.S. local governments is voluntary, and only a small segment of the public sector has successfully implemented them organization-wide. Often, a single department or division will entertain such an endeavor; therefore, the jurisdiction never fully reaps the benefits of a participatory, holistic performance management framework across the organization or community.

Aligning Resources and Activities with Corporate Goals

A major focus of all Audit Commission council assessments is whether the council is actively managing performance of services in line with its stated corporate goals and priorities. Over the years, councils have become better and better at articulating what those priorities are and ensuring that performance is managed against outcomes in a balanced way. The connection between performance measurement and the council's goals is sometimes called a *golden thread.*

Ideally, each individual's work should be aligned to unit and departmental objectives, which in turn are linked to corporate priorities. Councils have developed processes in their annual planning cycles to ensure alignment of departmental and divisional objectives with corporate priorities. Widespread usage of scorecards (balanced and otherwise) provides the framework for maintaining multi-tiered performance updates driven by real-time, milestone reporting.

In the United States, a formalized approach to alignment that requires third-party evaluation of goals, objectives, and performance is not common. Often, U.S. local governments try to tie performance to their budgets, but that is where the effort ends. Service Efforts and Accomplishments (SEA) reporting, promoted by the Government Accounting Standards Board (GASB), provides a structured format for aligning performance results with priorities. And some communities (such as Maricopa County, Arizona; Charlotte, North Carolina; and Prince William County, Virginia) go to great lengths to internally ensure resource and goal alignment.

Benchmarking against Similar Profile Organizations

From an early point, the need to compare one's own performance with others has been paramount in assessing U.K. councils' progress. This benchmarking is considerably more practical in the United Kingdom than in the United States, because all U.K. councils are required every year to submit results to the Audit Commission on the same set of mandatory performance indicators. These data are then published online at www.audit-commission.gov.uk, where they may be downloaded for further analysis.

Progressive councils wanting to do more with benchmark data found the annual data update too retrospective, and the data didn't necessarily include organizations of a similar profile and size. So many formed their own benchmark peer groups, started using software to gather data regularly, and produced more frequent performance reports.

By contrast, U.S. local governments don't use a common set of performance measures, making sound comparisons amongst peers problematic. A number of benchmarking initiatives have developed, such as the International City/County Management Association (ICMA) and the Florida

Benchmarking Consortium, but they face a number of challenges. Many entities do not understand the concept of benchmarking; it is difficult to ensure that participants use consistent data collection techniques or to access data for a similarly profiled peer group; and the cost to participate in benchmarking groups may be prohibitive. Nonetheless, most local governments that participate in these benchmarking exercises still find the efforts valuable.

Performance Reporting to Citizens

Visit any U.K. local government website, and you will find a variety of performance reports informing citizens about the council's progress toward achieving targets. Both corporate and departmental/service-based data are available. The performance plans that are required annually as part of the regulatory regime present, in some detail, results relative to benchmark peer groups and aligned to corporate goals and objectives.

Often, reports are posted in a PDF format, but a growing number of councils directly publish data from their performance management software to their websites. These reports are generally interactive and visually engaging, displaying traffic-lighted gauges and trend charts that allow the citizen to drill down for more detail. By contrast, U.S. local government websites typically contain very little service performance information, aside from what might be buried in the annual budget document. Fewer still have strong visual presentation of performance results, let alone any dynamic facilities for citizens to drill down for further details.

Tracking Performance in Partnerships

Local governments rely on a variety of other public bodies to fully deliver local-priority outcomes. For some time now, U.K. councils have had to extend performance management to cover the work done by partnerships. When multiple organizations are involved, each with varying degrees of accountability, coordinating partnership action plans and performance measurement is a major challenge. U.K. councils formalize their multiple partnerships in a local strategic partnership (LSP) body that is responsible for developing and implementing a local area agreement (LAA). Many councils have developed internal skills to address the major issues, such as ensuring consistent information management across multiple organizations; managing performance indicators, risks, and action plans; and reporting performance in terms of both the individual organizations' and the partner body's priorities.

In the United States, intergovernmental coordination, let alone partnerships with non-governmental agencies, does not appear to have the same level of dedicated management direction as with U.K. councils. Perhaps the greatest difference is the ability to share management information on performance across multiple organizations—despite sharing similar goals and outcomes. The lack of mandatory performance achievement hinders improvement in U.S. local government partnership performance.

Using Software to Support the Performance Management Process

In response to their rigorous mandatory performance requirements, U.K. councils turned to performance measurement software to streamline reporting processes and deliver other efficiencies. Software is U.K. councils' fundamental tool for engaging staff in performance management and ensuring a consistent approach to measurement and reporting across the organization and in partnerships. Analysis shows that U.K. local government has the highest adoption rates for performance management software in the world. More than 75 percent of U.K. councils use a packaged solution, as opposed to spreadsheet software such as Microsoft® Excel or an in-house solution.

By contrast, we estimate that at best five percent of U.S. local governments use a packaged solution, with a similar number relying on in-house systems—leaving approximately 90 percent of U.S. local governments using nothing or just Excel.

Within U.K. local governments, there is generally little support for the regulatory regime and the way it controls how councils operate. Nonetheless, despite the unpopularity of the Audit Commission's requirements, few would dispute that they have led to better quality measurement. Importantly, those who ultimately pay for these entities—citizens—typically have much better access to relevant performance information in the United Kingdom than in the United States. The challenge of getting citizens in both countries more involved with that information, and using it as a trigger for action, remains.

Discussion Questions

1. Identify and discuss the mission of the U.K. Audit Commission.

2. Why is the concept of performance measurement more advanced in the U.K. than in the U.S.?

3. Identify and discuss the concept of BVPI. What is the purpose and benefit of these indicators?

4. What is the golden thread?

5. Compare benchmarking in the U.S. and the U.K., highlighting the major differences.

6. Compare performance reporting and the use of performance measures software in the U.S. and the U.K., highlighting the major differences.

Index

Performance Networks: Transforming Governance for the 21st Century
Lynn Sandra Kahn, PhD

This book provides roadmaps and guidelines for executives, managers, and team leaders who are accountable for results in the new world of interagency networks that aim to deliver measurable results across traditional boundaries. The author presents ten "views" of performance networks, adapted from current, successful, multi-agency partnerships; these views provide specific guidance on transformational strategic planning to deliver better results.

ISBN 978-1-56726-242-1 ■ Product Code B421 ■ 164 pages

Plain Language in Government Writing: A Step-by-Step Guide
Judith Gillespie Myers, PhD

Whether you're in the public or private sector, good writing skills are critical to your success in the workplace. This book shows you how to apply federal plain-language guidelines to every type of writing — from emails, memos, and letters to agency communications, technical procedures, and budget justification statements. Through numerous exercises as well as examples from a variety of federal and state agencies this practical guide walks you step-by-step through every phase of the writing process, providing tips for improved clarity, conciseness, and completeness.

ISBN 978-1-56726-224-7 ■ Product Code B247 ■ 430 pages

Governmental and Nonprofit Financial Management
Charles K. Coe, PhD

The first resource to comprehensively discuss both governmental and nonprofit financial management! This book makes it easy for both nonprofit and governmental managers to understand essential governmental and nonprofit financial management topics and their various subfields.

ISBN 978-1-56726-183-7 ■ Product Code B837 ■ 321 pages

Strategic Leadership: The General's Art
Mark Grandstaff, PhD, and Georgia Sorenson, PhD

This book provides aspiring leaders with an understanding of the behavior and competencies that make a good strategic leader. It teaches leaders how to think strategically in a volatile, uncertain environment and thereby provide transformational leadership and to shape outcomes With contributions from senior military leaders as well as experts in the fields of strategic leadership, systems and critical thinking, and corporate culture, this invaluable reference shows readers how to move from mid-level manager to strategic-thinking senior executive.

ISBN 978-1-56726-236-0 ■ Product Code B360 ■ 335 pages